THE PLANNING PROCRASTINATING PERFECTIONIST

A Simple Guide to Get Out of Your Head and Into Your Life!

DANTE MOORE

Copyright © 2025 by Dante Moore

All rights reserved.

No part of this publication may be reproduced, stored in a retrieval system, or transmitted in any form or by any means—electronic, mechanical, photocopying, recording, or otherwise—without the prior written permission of the author, except in the case of brief quotations used in articles or reviews with credit cited.

This book is a work of nonfiction. The insights, strategies, and personal experiences shared are true to the best of the author's knowledge and are intended to encourage, equip, and empower readers who struggle with procrastination, overplanning, and perfectionism. The goal is to help individuals move from ideas into action, break free from limiting cycles, and build clarity, courage, and consistency in their personal and professional lives.

Cover Design: Mila. M
Illustrator: Illustrations by Tom Chain
Edited By: Georgina Chong-You
Photography: Yack Shack Media

ISBN: 979-8-9932172-0-8
Printed in the United States of America
First Edition: 2025

Published by: Era 11 Publishing Inc.

For more information or to contact the author, visit:
www.iamdantemoore.com

"For every dreamer who's been stuck in their own head — this is your release."

This book is for all the overthinkers and dreamers who are finally ready to be unleashed into the world. It's for my inner child and yours, acting as a bold whisper to become exactly who they've always imagined themselves to be.

And it is especially inspired by a man of high honor, noble character, and unforgettable authenticity, who lived his potential in full view for the benefit of so many. To my late Uncle, Vernest C. Moore — you are forever my inspiration and guide. I love you, Uncle V.

IAMDANTEMOORE.COM

Table of Contents

INTRODUCTION | In Full Transparency. 1

CHAPTER 01 | Start With You 7

CHAPTER 02 | Potential Is Disgusting 35

CHAPTER 03 | The Theory of Moore 55

CHAPTER 04 | The Planning 79

CHAPTER 05 | Are You Full Yet? 91

CHAPTER 06 | The Procrastination 105

CHAPTER 07 | No One 115

CHAPTER 08 | What Are You Thinking? 123

CHAPTER 09 | The Perfectionism 131

CHAPTER 10 | If You Scared, Say You Scared 141

CHAPTER 11 | Progress Over Perfection 161

CHAPTER 12 | You Are Unstoppable 177

CHAPTER 13 | Serious or Delirious? 195

CHAPTER 14 | End With Them 207

About the Author. 217

INTRODUCTION

In Full Transparency

They say the first step in solving a problem is admitting you have one. So here it goes... *Hello! My name is Dante Moore, and I am a* **Planning Procrastinating Perfectionist**. I'm sure I've had this long-term condition for over 28 years. I don't say this with pride, but with vulnerability and introspection.

Now, you are most likely wondering why I chose to write a book about my life as a procrastinator. Sure, I've felt stuck, but I thought there was more to it than pure laziness or lack of ambition. My procrastination had been sandwiched between building plans for years and my need for it to be perfect before being released. I'd never read anything that addressed the nuances of procrastinators like me, and honestly, I didn't think I'd be courageous enough to even get this far. The good news is that I created the title of this book nearly 10 years ago, and I am finally getting around to working on it. I guess that's fitting behavior for my self-diagnosis in a way. I said to myself when the idea struck me that this work of mine would be a catalyst for others to finally unburden themselves and feel heard and seen in the spaces that they were in.

I made whole-hearted declarations to myself that compiling, writing, and publishing this book would be all the tangible proof I needed. The proof that I was no longer in this prolonged stage of constantly **planning** to do something while **procrastinating** daily into being crippled by my **perfectionist** attitude. So finally, here we are…today with a finished product. Hell yea! Take that, you stupid condition.

Your "Cure" is in the Creation

For many years, I was confined to the realm of my own creativity and ideas. If you are reading this book, it is tangible proof that there's a light at the end of the tunnel. I can honestly now say that I'm free from the debilitating state of overanalyzing my thoughts, ideas, and plans which has held me captive for decades. But let's be honest and set realistic expectations, because being cured of this is close to impossible, as that's not how life works. I like to view this work that I'm doing as more of a lifelong treatment plan, to which I am ever recovering with one actionable step at a time. I suppose this is a healing journey that allows me to remain a constant work in progress, further regenerating the whole parts of myself with each step forward. Admittedly, I've still got a ton of work to do. Countless hours turned into years spent wondering how my words would land on the pages, all while second-guessing myself as others around me were taking their big chances. It has been mentally exhausting, comparatively envious, and simultaneously exasperating. I want to say that this book is evidence that I was truly made for more than just having good ideas – and so are you, my friend!

How did I get to this point of finally creating? How did I get unbound from all the potential locked in my 3-P condition, as I have now coined it? I needed to get out of my comfort zone and my environment first, because all the familiar things around me were so grey and dull. Deeply repetitive cycles that were uninspiring, cyclical, and underwhelming. So, I booked a solo trip to Denver and locked myself in a hotel room until this book was birthed out of me. That's right, a Philadelphia native took a spontaneous flight to the Colorado mountains for the first time to spend four days just existing and writing. I wanted to hone in on my creativity and finally dispel the illness of my own stifled genius, which had been exacerbated by the overindulgent assurance that I needed perfect circumstances to thrive. I did it and I did it ugly!

My outside life was in shambles as I was recently released from employment during the resurgence of a Global Pandemic, while in isolation and battling through a divorce. My perfect life had been blown up, so what else did I have left but to produce what had been building within me? Perhaps many things that previously prohibited me from going all in were just beautiful distractions.

At the time of writing this, I am in the later years of my thirties and have had the privilege of starting and running some amazing projects! I had been responsible for starting businesses, building organizations, and leading people in diverse team settings. I've discovered that I'm gifted in being able to communicate effectively, train and coach others, and map out strategic visions with intent and purpose. My journey has taken me to sit among a diverse group of people, helping them become their best selves by unlocking their potential, devising strategies for their dreams, and enhancing their overall performance.

To this end, I see my role clearly defined as an **Insight Extraction Coach & Strategist**. I help people and leaders just like you, pull clarity from chaos, and turn hidden potential into strategies and action that create real growth and lasting results.

Now, imagine doing that for everyone else, all while your very own treasures remained buried, awaiting the "perfect" time to be unearthed. I'll admit that this dichotomy has become a torturous yet fulfilling existence. And you, have you continually been pouring out to nourish others while convincing yourself that the same wellspring isn't ready for you to drink and be filled by too? I was content and even felt validated as I helped others fulfill their dreams and received compliments from them of my talent and gifts. Then they began questioning why I had not fully stepped out to be who I was made to be by using these same gifts and talents to invest in myself first. I'd usually sit and proudly self-loathe and tell them about all the perfect ideas I had planned and then give them a justifiable reason as to why now was just 'not the right time.'

Why am I sharing this with you? To show you that I not only understand it, but I have lived it. It's never easy when you have all the pieces but still lack the finished product, is it? Even though I've had small wins and great moments, it's the big stuff— those ideas and dreams that keep you awake at night. That kind of passion you could talk about for hours, and it feels like only minutes pass. It's that thing you confide only in your closest people, and even then, you don't share the full idea because it's sacred. Those deep desires to do more and be more, feeling like the road was made just for you. We cherish those things, which might be why we lock them away and bury them deep, hoping to protect them. These are the things that make me feel most free, as they've been imprisoned and hidden from the world—and even from myself. There, they remain chained to the doubts and fears inside my mind.

But you are not alone, and I am here to partner with you to help get you out of this rut. This book is for you. It is for me. It is for all of us stuck in our own heads with a great concept that never matured outside of our minds and into something tangible.

The hard work is the heart work here. This will not be easy as it requires you to rework the psychology of your brain, the motivations of your heart, the disciplines of your hands, and the language of your lips. If you're anything like me, you may view this book as a self-help guide that you'll skim through and turn to only the chapters whose titles interest you. Or maybe you'll use it as a literature to study and quote to your friends as another notch in your belt of the books you've read this year. Perhaps, it may sit on your bookshelf as an accessory with the cover art front-facing. But those actions only bring you right back to where you started and keep you stuck doing nothing.

My goal is to help you understand with an open mind and an honest look at who you currently are, why you are in your current position, and ways to get out of it, while also activating you immediately. The intention here is that you don't leave with a bunch of lofty ideas, but a purposeful guide to help you get into action. No one will be able to do this work for you;

however, my aim is to be a guide to assist you until the finish line. This book is designed to help you enjoy the process as much as you enjoyed the planning. It has been developed to help you run after, with tenacity and poise, the passions that have been sidelined. I will use many real-life examples with brutal transparency to show you how I've walked the talk, and it's not just you who has battled through 3-P. I'm not a guru, I'm just a goer!

This work we are getting into is not just business, it's personal – deeply personal. It's a swift kick in the ass to remind you of who you are and what you are holding onto. None of us has it all together, and nothing is perfect; however, **done** is better than *thinking* about doing.

So, grab a pen, a highlighter, stickies, write in the margins, fold the pages... do whatever you need to do. Get ugly with it and get into it. Don't you dare skip a page or force a chapter. Take your time and proceed in order as needed. We will not cheat this moment by jumping in halfway; instead, use this launchpad to help you start acting on the greatness that lives within. I believe you are made for this, and I'm rooting for you to be uniquely you and give birth to the thing that you have been protecting for far too long.

Let's get to work!

Signed, (your guide and friend)
Dante Moore

CHAPTER 01

Start With You

It's not me, it's you! Really, we are often the problem that gets in our own way. I think 90s R&B group SWV said it best in their song "Weak," when they sang, *"I can't figure out just what to do, when the cause and cure is you."* With respect, the cause (and the cure) to your dilemma is simply--**You**. The best and worst news you can hear is that it all starts with you. On one end, it can be empowering to know that you are in full control of what happens in your life as it relates to your deepest desires and your drive.

I felt it fitting to begin the first chapter of this book as an exercise in **self-examination**. We always start a process of transformation with ourselves because you must hold yourself accountable for the execution and the results, or the lack thereof. You owe it to your untold story and your unlocked destiny to get yourself in check. Yet, we often struggle to examine ourselves—our hearts, motives, and even our failures.

Consistent self-examination and brutal objectivity will be critical to you finally getting out of the way and making a way for yourself. If you haven't started yet, that means a part of you is holding you back. A piece that we will examine thoroughly in the procrastination and perfectionism sections. Checking yourself means being honest about where you are and what has been holding you back – even if it's yourself. Words and phrases have meanings, so remember to use them accordingly and with prudence. You'll need to be introspective here, examining your skills, motivations, and behaviors, as well as the things you've left undone. Examination for you will lead to discovery because there are invisible arenas deep within you that you may not even know exist. This is why extraction is necessary.

Examine Yourself

Now, I am a huge advocate for words of affirmation and self-care practices. How we talk to ourselves matters for our healing and growth. It's part of how we train our hearts and minds. What we believe and know to be true about ourselves plays a pivotal role in how we present ourselves in our day-to-day interactions. Yet, with the responsibility of embracing our humanity, it's important that we leave room for unbiased hard truths to be factored in as well. We need to see and hear the truth about ourselves to evolve and mature into the people we aspire to be.

Our current social climate however tends to lean too heavily against this self-affirmation mindset, creating a vacuum where many have decided to subscribe to the "talk to me nicely" ideology. We filter out what we don't like and mute those who are too tough on us. No one wants to hear the bad; they want to hear only the good. The result? We remain stuck in a state of ignorance, snuggling under the layers of alternative buzzwords, giving grace to our excuses, removing those who are too judgmental, and labeling every environment that doesn't coddle our comfort as "toxic." Again, I'm not against positive self-affirmations at all. In fact, as a certified neuroscience coach, I am aware that whatever you say out loud is deposited into your subconscious as earnest truth and rewires your brain. Affirmations tend to force us into motion, while simultaneously we avoid certain truths about ourselves and our choices in an effort to avoid that which we know we have to do.

Like most good things, when stretched to extremes, it results in a culture and mindset that is an echo chamber, submissive only to its own authority. Leaning too far to either side of apathy or hyper offense can grant us the same resolve on either end – arrested development. We need to find balance, my friends, and to do that, we need to be rational and somewhat pragmatic.

Most things in life exist on a spectrum where the **delicacy of diversity and the cohesion of contrast** rest.

At times, it may be challenging to handle deep, constructive critiques concerning our craft or character. But avoidance will only cause you to be stuck there. So, starting with you means making the heart work a priority. All your life choices, your successes, and your failures all start with you and what you allow. When you begin doing the hard work, you will reveal what is behind the creativity you've been suffocating for too long. But first, you have to get out of your own head!

You are not a victim of your environment, your upbringing, or your traumas. I know firsthand how external factors and life's forces can convince you that your worth should be sidelined. This is regressive thinking, which we often don't recognize until it's too late and the prime years have gone by. You can and will be a conqueror of those things because although they are part of your journey, they are not the end of it. You are still here and persevering. Stop allowing single incidents to define you and shape you into being a different version of yourself that you aren't satisfied with.

I want to explore some of the common barriers that are holding you back and keeping you stuck in your head, away from the life you desire. Unclear goals, a lack of self-awareness, projected fears, unhealthy comparisons, misaligned environments, unidentified behavior patterns, unused skills, and core competencies. The method of identifying and unlocking concealed areas, while filtering out the true essence of yourself, is what is known as the **Hard Work + Heart Work Method (HWork2)**. It is grueling, but also insightful, because when it is completed, you no longer need to wait for someone to tell you about yourself; you can simply apply what you know about yourself to the work of your hands. We'll discuss this method further, and I will guide you through its application in later chapters. Currently, I'd like to discuss the science of self-awareness.

When in conversation with my therapist, close friends, and loved ones, I strive to discuss myself and my life with a great deal of objectivity. In that safe space, as a practice, I decipher (as best as I can) all my feelings within my experiences while attempting to use my skills of compartmentalizing to see clearly. This displays a level of self-awareness, but it is a muscle I have had to learn to develop over time, and there is still much room for improvement. I'd like to introduce you to a unique tool for working it out for yourself. This is my first gift to you, as we begin our journey together...

The Johari Window

The Johari Window of self-awareness is a powerful tool for understanding oneself and others. It is a simple, yet effective technique built in a 4-quadrant model to enhance self-awareness and help you build trust.

Each of us has these four areas in life:

Open Area: Information known to others and to us. (The Arena)

Hidden Area: Information known to us and not others. (The Facade)

Blind Spot: Information known to others and not us.

Unknown: Information unknown to both us and others.

Before you can think about understanding others, you must ask: What do you really know about yourself? I'm not talking about your aspirations or ideas, but truly who **you** are. There are areas in your life that are blind spots to you for a myriad of reasons that others can see quite clearly. This is where openness and humility to hear trusted objective input is important. Territories exist in your life right now that you are hiding from everyone with the facade and the cloak of your choice and that may be your hindrance. There are other sectors inside of you that are lying dormant, unbeknownst to you and the outside world, and all it takes is a spark to ignite them from the unknown to the actual.

You may pause and ask yourself why this is important and essential for me? Because your ideas, dreams, visions, and passions do not live outside of you or apart from you just yet. They are still in your head and heart, just swirling around, and often confused with who you are. Therefore, if you are real with yourself about where you are in life, you can also be ambitious about the things inside of you that you want produced out of life. This helps you beat anyone to the punch that may try to define where you are incorrectly, because you've rehearsed truth-telling to yourself already. **A lack of self-awareness and an inability to acknowledge your identity may result in submitting to a fantasy with an undeveloped idea.** You cannot create anything clear for others to receive from a mind of chaos and confusion.

This is a healthy and crucial step in your journey. Start with **You**. Your idea(s) are extensions of you, birthed and incubated in the recesses of your heart and mind. Thus, if you live in a world where you cannot be honest with yourself about sharp truths that define your current state of being, then, unfortunately, your ideas will stay just as attached to that delusion and remain dreams. How you see yourself is how you will communicate and cultivate your ideas. If you live in a fantasy to avoid pain and hurt, then, consequently, your ideas will be chained to a beautiful utopia where nothing can go wrong, and outside of that place, they will cease to exist. This is the type of thinking we want to address immediately and leave behind.

Know Yourself

My first challenge is for you to be honest with yourself. Take a moment and write down some truths about yourself from an objective standpoint. (*At the end of this chapter, I will help you create your Self-Awareness window through the heart work compass.*) For example, when administering assessments or conducting interviews, professionals often ask the same questions in different ways to elicit the most honest and accurate answers from the participant. They are seeking a level of consistency and alignment, regardless of how the question is posed. This would indicate a person not only is aware of themselves but is even subconsciously consistent in their truths.

The second challenge is to know yourself deeply and intimately. This is what I call being in touch with yourself. For instance, let's consider a question that is often asked during small talk: "How are you?" Most times, our immediate response is, "I'm good." That's a reflex that is embedded in us. It's reflexive, not reflective, because most of the time we are mentally on autopilot. Even if we are good, there may be a more suitable answer for that question, but it takes too much mental anguish to drum it up, so we haphazardly throw out "I'm good." However, I'd like to encourage you to think deeper and look at what this question could actually be asking:

- What has occurred in your life since the last time I've seen/spoken to you?
- How are you really feeling?
- What are some of the things that are making you feel this way?
- Considering those things and how you feel, do you believe you have the power to change them to generate new outcomes?

All these questions could be wrapped up in "how are you" but most of us won't get to the five layers deep of developmental probing questions to unearth how we truly are. As a result, we settle for "I'm fine" or "I'm good" when we all know that's simply not the full truth. Perhaps we think that others won't care enough to hear all about what is going on with us. We've got a few emotions swirling around that we haven't quite got out yet. Maybe we believe that our feelings are invalid and don't have a place in that conversation. We may even be in a place where we haven't given enough thought to answer that question fully with awareness and clarity.

These are all obstacles that keep our most authentic selves hidden from the outside world. Think critically for a moment, if given the stage with the question of 'how are you' to answer five layers deep, could you? Could you answer all those questions posed above? Would you be able to freely and uninhibitedly

> *Your feelings are directly tied to your daily progress and habits.*

express the feelings that you have? Would that even be a desire for you, or would you feel too odd and disconnected from yourself to answer? Perhaps it's even too vulnerable a space for you to even want to answer. Remember, in that moment, if you choose to shrug it off as not a big deal or unimportant, that speaks volumes to the thing you've been working on as well. If you can't or won't elaborate on your own person, how far do you think you will get when asked about your deepest passions, longings, and ideas?

It's time to work those muscles again! I believe in the phrase "practice makes permanent," and we must practice regularly being in touch with ourselves. Every day, you aren't going to feel like diving five layers deep, but you do need to check in with yourself. For this, one of the tools I use while journaling is the Feelings Wheel, which we will get to shortly. However, the practice didn't just come out of thin air; I had to actually understand my emotions first before I could verbalize my feelings about that emotion.

It's impossible to be honest about your goals when you can't even be honest with yourself because you don't know what is going on in your mind. Can anyone relate? All these things come at you so fast in life, and they trigger you in different ways, and some of us just react. Some of us are left feeling "some kind of way," as they say, but we never took the time to explore what that way actually was. In my facilitation of classes in this regard, I realized many of us were never taught by our paternal examples how to discover this. However, we are grown now, and we do ourselves a disservice when we don't work through the emotions we have; often, it is because we are still ill-equipped. I don't accept that you don't have the language to express your emotions through feelings. The language exists; we just have to learn it. I believe we just lack the tools and the implementation of how to use them to navigate life's challenges and overcome the difficult feelings that have us stuck.

First, let's decipher the difference between emotions and feelings. They both play a crucial role in how humans perceive and respond to the world around them. We will start with emotions as they are the foundation from which feelings flow. Now, stay with me for a minute; this will all play a crucial role in getting the good juice out of you, but we've got to go through the press first!

Emotions

While there is no scientific consensus around the definition of emotions, we can use the following. According to the American Psychological Association (APA), emotion is defined as "a complex reaction pattern, involving experiential, behavioral and physiological elements." Emotions are how individuals deal with matters or situations they find personally significant.

There is neuroscience, which reveals that emotions can hit you without warning or welcome and affect every part of your being. Involuntary reactions occur automatically to universal stimuli. This is called a trigger. Emotions become the filter for everything we think and do. Let's look further in education and illustration as to how this universal and biological wiring of emotions works itself out from its objective arrival to our subjective interpretation.

In 1980, psychologist Robert Plutchik created the wheel of emotions to visualize the complexity of emotions and help people identify and label them. Plutchik stated first however that there are 8 basic emotions:

1. Anger
2. Anticipation
3. Joy
4. Trust
5. Fear
6. Surprise
7. Sadness
8. Disgust

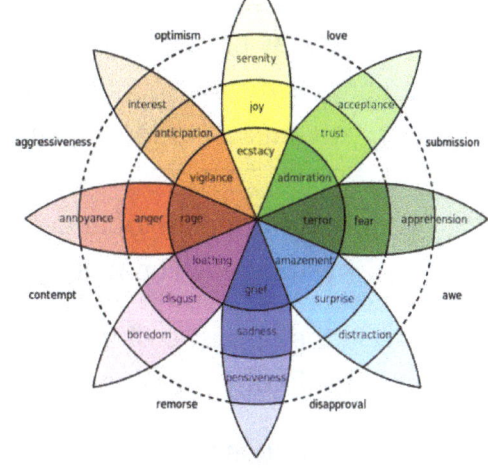

Plutchik developed the wheel of emotions to help understand the complex and nuanced nature of our emotions, the various relationships among them, and the intensity and degrees to which they occur. The Emotion Wheel uses color to depict discrete emotions and blends of emotion. It uses their gradients to express intensity, and uses the geometric shape to reflect the polarity (or similarity) of emotions. The wheel in turn, due to its complexity, opens up to a greater extent to look like a lotus flower. It is a great tool to help people communicate and regulate their emotions, along with the awareness of the root causes of behavior.

Remember, emotions are closely coordinated with the body's physiological responses. So even when you are burying your emotions, your body and behaviors will still tell on you and inform others through your facial, verbal, and/or behavioral expressions. Have you ever found yourself turning your face up or making a noise in light of something you were displeased by or overexcited with? If you examine below, these are based on the physiological reaction each emotion creates in animals and humans according to Plutchik's research:

Hint: When we say physiology here, that means the way you, as a living organism, and your body parts function, considering something you encountered, aka stimuli. Don't overthink this.

- Fear is the opposite of anger.
    - » **Physiology:** Get small and hide vs get big and loud
- Joy is the opposite of sadness.
    - » **Physiology:** Connect vs withdraw
- Anticipation is the opposite of surprise.
    - » **Physiology:** Examine closely vs jump back
- Disgust is the opposite of trust.
    - » **Physiology:** Reject vs Embrace

Here would be the linear progression of how our emotions work by nature:

Stimulus → perception → emotion → physiological change → impulse → action/reaction → behavior

In this way, when emotions arise, we are no different from any other animal that is operating under an adaptive response for survival. How long have you just been in survival mode and moving with whatever was thrown at you? It's not enough to identify that something occurred that you recognized and didn't like, then elicited the emotion of anger, and you felt your heart rate rise, causing you to react. This is short-sighted and is not optimal for maximizing all that you are. Some may even describe this behavior as low-vibrational, and for good reason. Most people that you come across, unfortunately, operate in this way because they haven't done the hard work of starting with themselves first. Consider these responses instead:

> REFLECT not REFLEX.
> RESPOND not REACT.

You are made for more than just being triggered and acting irrationally. We need to thoughtfully deal with what just impacted us, and this is where feelings come into play.

Feelings

Feelings are a way we consciously and subjectively do the cognitive work to interpret complex emotions that exist on a spectrum.

Feelings are our learned responses to emotional triggers. Learned responses that are shaped by our individual beliefs, thoughts, and worldviews. Feelings are not often automatic, involuntary responses, but they are associations of the former that we have learned in relation to our emotions.

One of the big parts here is that the subjective feeling component of the processing refers to our experience of emotions. Everyone can experience the same event at the same time, and it can trigger the same core emotion, but how each individual feels in response to that emotion varies from case to case.

I saw this firsthand, when my Philadelphia Eagles won the Super Bowl against the Kansas City Chiefs in 2025, during the halftime show with Kendrick Lamar, we all experienced the same event in the stadium. Our core emotion of anticipation was all the same prior to the start of the performance. Yet, when I looked around as it progressed onward, I saw a change in different emotions and expressed feelings from each crowd goer. For those of us who are more "melanated" and aware of the deeper messages, we were locked in with anticipation and joy, dissecting the performance. Others who were just fans responded with excitement and yelled some of the popular lyrics. Then there was a litany of people who remained, and they were expressionless, perplexed, and some even slightly offended, dare I say disgusted, that this was the selected headliner for the show.

One event, different emotions, entirely different feelings, all based on things that are learned and programmed in prior for each person. In the days to come, I unpacked the layers of the performance and its significance with several friends, discussing how we felt about it. However, for the average attendee, who doesn't understand the amount of time and effort invested in a performance like this one, they may have dismissed it as boring and uneventful, which would have caused them to miss the artistry and the message woven in.

With this knowledge, you can now unpack the often-quoted phrase *FEEL your FEELINGS*.

FEEL (individually interpret and respond to)
YOUR (from a subjective stance)
FEELINGS (the core emotion that triggered a physiological response and has you ready to react).

No wonder so many of us get the words emotions and feelings entangled so often! I told you words carry meaning, and not understanding them can cripple your communication with yourself and others.

The lesson: some people can see opportunity where others only see obstacles. The danger in not starting with you is that you may fall into the comparison game. Measuring how a person who looks like you, who is from your area, with the same access, has accomplished what you may not be able to – YET! The difference is that one person took the time to not just react to triggers, but to work through how it impacted them, then respond with intention so their true feelings helped to shape their future behaviors.

Observe what happens on the linear progression when you take the extra time for your feelings:

Stimulus → (pre-conceived) perception → emotion → physiological change → impulse → identify true feelings → respond in action → behavior

---

What a powerful game changer this can be! All of this wrapped up in your feelings? Who would've thought it?

Now, of course, I won't just leave you to try to figure out how to process feelings without any help. Remember, earlier I stated that "I don't accept that you don't have the language to put around your feelings." Since I don't accept that, I will help you extract the words needed to put a pin on what you are feeling, and we will do that by finally getting to the Feelings Wheel.

Although Robert Plutchik laid the groundwork for understanding emotions, it was Gloria Wilcox in 1982 who first elaborated on this concept with the feelings wheel. I like to believe that this feelings wheel is the literary diction of our emotions to help people communicate most effectively the state they are in. Throughout the years, Willcox's wheel has gone through several upgrades and iterations from an English Teacher, Kaitlin Robbs, Vocabulary Wheel of feelings in 2014 that she called the 'wheel of words'. All the way to where it finally rested on what I believe to be the most expansive and visually pleasing emotional wheel developed in 2015 by Geoffrey Roberts.

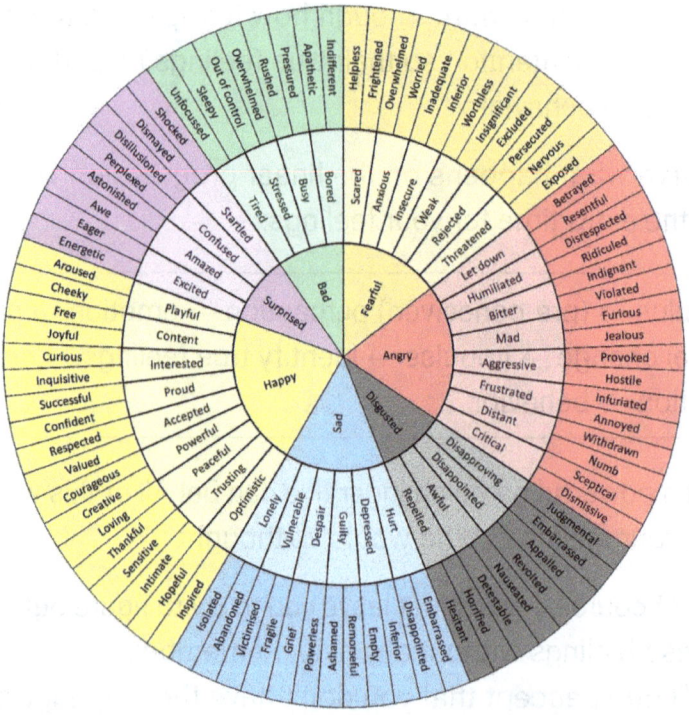

Here is the Geoffrey Roberts Emotional Wheel, which I call the **FEELINGS WHEEL,** which starts with the core emotions closest to the center. You'll notice some of the 8 have been grouped into one and there are word replacements for others. Nonetheless, this singular tool acts as a powerful measure for checking in with yourself any time you get that gut feeling that something is off, and you can't quite express it. Before you react to whatever you have made up in your mind from that which you may be experiencing, take a moment and list out several feelings to flesh it all out. With this tool, I want you to revisit the questions at the beginning of this section and see how much more equipped you will be to answer them now. Do you see the power in knowing thyself? You can now go five layers deep in questions about how you are simply because you know a little bit more about how to interpret who you are and what you feel.

Let's take a quick pause here. You're doing a great job! So, how do you feel lol?

I'd like to give you a real activity now that will be imperative for you to start answering for yourself. When I say answer yourself, that means write it down somewhere, anywhere. It can be directly inside the book, and if you need more space, consider using a journal or the notes app on your phone. If you just read them and skip answering, you are only cheating your future. I hope these next few questions will serve you just as well as they have for me. I learned to think this way from the late Dr. Myles Munroe, a prolific teacher and speaker. He posits that every human being on the planet, at one point, comes to ask themselves these five basic questions:

1. Who am I? (Identity)
2. Where am I from? (Source)
3. Why am I here? (Purpose)
4. What do I possess? (Talents)
5. Where am I going? (Destiny)

Some of these questions may not have immediate, complete answers, and that is okay. Some of them will be met with "I don't know," and that's not ok. Here is why – because there are layers to these answers, so we have to at least *try* to start answering. Anything you write down is acceptable, and if you don't know where to even start, that demonstrates that you just need more guidance and tools. That's totally fine, and that may be part of what has you stuck, reading this book now. Don't worry, we'll do this together. Just make sure you have the mindset to want to know the answers for yourself.

For any unexplored area of ourselves, we should be curious to lean into. We need to be clear on who we are and what we want. **Free-flowing ideas about our passion and purpose cannot be born from a confused mind about our identity.** This bears repeating: your ideas do not live apart from you while still in the generation phase, so they need supreme brutal honesty about who the real **you** is.

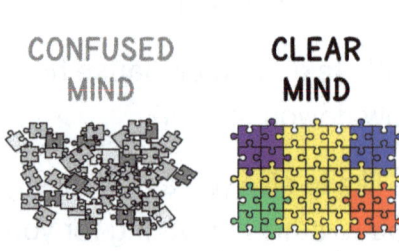

Invest in Yourself

I once had a colleague who made over six figures in his career and who would frequently discuss various business pursuits he wanted to consider in the future. He came to me and spoke about wanting to invest in a business idea he had heard someone else suggest, which would help him generate passive income, or what he called "some quick bread." Bread is a slang term for money. Anyway, intrigued as I often am, I followed up with a series of questions. I wasn't sure that he possessed the long-term vision and self-awareness to recognize his commitments and spending habits, allowing him to see an investment opportunity through until it matured.

I started by asking how often he frequented his favorite hookah lounge, where I already knew he spent a considerable amount of his leisure time. He stated that he went three to four times a week. Each time he spent roughly $30, which doesn't include any alcohol he purchases before getting to the location, because it's B.Y.O.B., or the gas it takes to drive there in his foreign car. On average, he was spending $120/week to smoke hookah (not including travel), which was $480/month. Without prompting, he shared with me that he also has to eat, and he should probably do better on that because he doesn't like to cook.

I asked him how much he spent on eating out each month. He stated, "An easy $3,200." I said to him, "You are paying half the rent of the hookah lounge by going as frequently as you go, aside from your food expenses." I went further and asked, "Have you considered maybe starting a hookah lounge yourself or going into business with someone? Perhaps even starting small by purchasing your own hookahs and renting them out." His answer, "Nah, I'm not really into it like that." I ended the conversation about investments there.

Here is a person who leaps at the word 'investment' without self-audit and lacks not only the knowledge but also the skills and discipline. Furthermore, anyone who mentions investment and fast cash in the same sentence is an automatic red flag for me. What was blind to him was known to me. I saw short-sightedness, habits of consumption, and a recipe for disaster for long-term investment. When I went layers deep in questions, to pivot to something more suitable to his lifestyle, notice how he reacted with an immediate lack of interest. Contradicting himself, his habits, and where he invests half of his most precious commodity (time) in the very same environment. This is an example of a person who lacks self-awareness and the ability to see an opportunity tailored to their true current self.

In this case, he was asking me about investing because he had a decent salary, and it may have sounded progressive to showcase his interest, given that he knows I'm an entrepreneur. However, he lacked the ability to identify an opportunity; he is already conditioned to have a fixed, convenient consumer mindset and is comfortable engaging in mindless activities for leisure instead of redistributing his income to make a profit. To top it all off, he is fully cognizant of the behaviors holding him back and yet remains crippled by it. Do you remember when we discussed the difference between those who merely react to life and those who respond? Here it is on full display, and it is all rooted in language and self-awareness.

The lesson from this example is this:

- Do a healthy examination of yourself before attempting to engage with an idea.
- Don't ever attempt to do business just because it sounds like the right thing.
- Avoid asking other people's opinions on something you have no intention of executing.

- Evaluate your capacity, steadfastness, coachability, and adaptability to change.
- Don't shrug off an opportunity to help you achieve what you said you wanted in a different form because it's not popular, you are unaware, or didn't think of it first.

One of the other key lessons I didn't add in would be **discipline**. I want to take a moment to discuss the impact of discipline and daily routines. In the above example, it is easy to point fingers and see how this person could have benefited from a more disciplined budget, business plan, and effective time management, among other things. It is much more difficult to do it for your own life because most of us have already armed ourselves with the justifiable ammo of excuses for why we aren't more efficient or, at best, more consistent.

If you are going to start with yourself, then you need to develop healthy habits, subconscious disciplines, and consistent routines. This is a crucial first step in maximizing your efficiency and shifting your mindset. Hijack your mind. Reward yourself for doing right by yourself. During the pandemic and going through my divorce, I invoked new routines. I had nothing but time and an empty home, so I started small with a gratitude routine, using daily sticky notes and a self-paced cognitive behavioral therapy app. I built that up over time to journaling and then disciplined myself to get a live therapist to see weekly.

A desired discipline to improve holistically helped me identify other areas of my life that needed attention. For me, it was easy to distract myself with work and new ventures, but that's not what I needed at the time. I needed to learn who I was transitioning into in this new season of my life. I prioritized health and wellness, and I noticed a change in my body, including the benefits to my skin and improved mobility. Adding on better budgeting and balanced travel to visit family to keep me from the lows of depression and loneliness, and reignite joy while giving me new ways to experience the world. I had a new rhythm to my life.

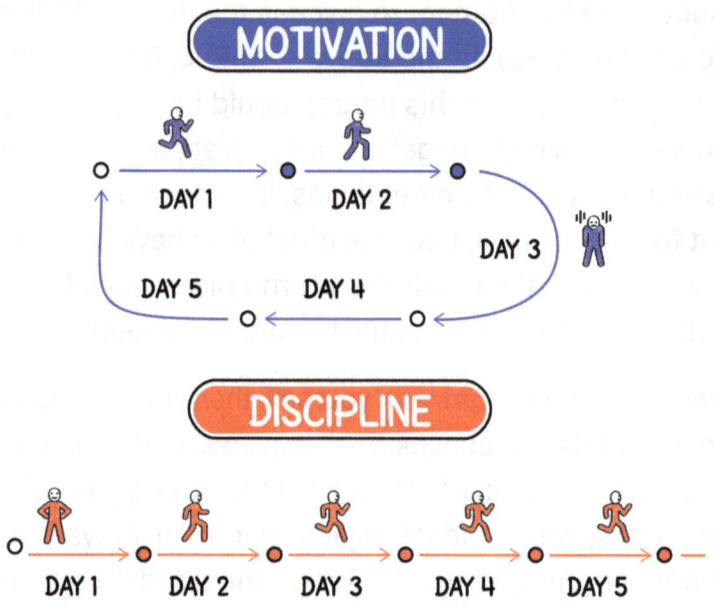

My disciplines have become my habits and, in turn, my daily routines. Compounded over time, this became a lifestyle. Motivation got me started, but discipline and consistency kept me. Now, I can't leave the house without my morning routine. It's a non-negotiable for me.

I recommend checking out the life-changing book "Atomic Habits" by James Clear. We don't gatekeep around here, so I will absolutely recommend dope resources from other writers that helped me. Friends of mine raved about it, so I caved and ordered it from Amazon. However, it sat on the shelf for over a year. Big surprise, right? I'm a (former) procrastinator. When I finally opened it, midway through establishing my own habits, it helped me push myself even further. This is another way we can care for ourselves, starting with ourselves and ensuring that whatever we undertake next, we are strong enough to handle and maintain. I was not too far or too big-headed to see that I needed more than my trials and errors. I too, needed help if I wanted to reach the next level of who I was becoming. When it comes to knowing yourself and holding yourself accountable, it's about being honest with knowing what you need. Self-deceit is not sexy but sad.

Be honest with yourself and know that just because you start a certain place doesn't mean you have to stay there. Honesty is the best policy for everything involving relationships, which includes your content, your creations, and your cravings. You need to complete a S.W.O.T (Strengths, Weaknesses, Opportunities, & Threats) analysis on yourself. Traditionally, these are used for businesses, but we are starting with you, right?

So, let's ask the questions. What are your Strengths, Weaknesses, Opportunities for growth, and Threats to that growth? This is vital to the success of any health or life initiative you may have. The plans may sound good in your mind and to your inner circle, but have you ever stopped to consider that the biggest hindrance may be you or your beautiful distractions? You need to chart this all out and get it settled once and for all. Through the HWork2 Method, it should help guide you in finding your strengths and underlying passions to apply immediately with specificity. I

> **Make your growth non-negotiable.**

took the long way to find out who I really was but now that I know, it's a passion to lead other people to the resources that helped me.

Your idea, when it comes to you, is yours solely, and if given the correct environment to thrive, it will be successful. However, you must give it the room it needs to grow and perform the necessary surgery on yourself to be that fertile ground.

In my early 20s, I would conjure up ideas left and right, and I would seldom tell anyone. I was afraid that someone would steal my idea and make it big off my original plans. What I wasn't acknowledging outwardly was that others would only be positioned to do that if I was in my own way stalling the execution. All due to my lack of preparedness and limited beliefs, I simply remained stuck in my head.

Hear me clearly, everyone has an idea or so they think – you are not special in that way. If the idea is unique, well thought out and able to be communicated, anyone with determination and poise may be able to see it through. Therefore, what do you add that makes this your idea and **your** thing if it's not directly revolving around your lived experience?

Furthermore, if it is so great, instead of sharing it with the world, why have you locked it away in the depths of your creative consciousness? Could it be that you are the ideas biggest enemy by your lack of self-reflection and awareness of your capacity or insecurities? The idea is great, but not greater than you – not yet, at least. Don't make the mistake of prioritizing it over yourself because it will only travel as far as you can go and are built to last so start with you.

Can I take this a step further? I believe ideas are alive and come from a source. This isn't just some theory I hold; ideas are always present, and they go to the person ready to bring them to life. If you're not preparing yourself to be a good incubator for these ideas, I firmly believe that because of your neglect, delay, self-abandonment, or irresponsibility, the idea will leave you and go somewhere else. Ironically, greats like Michael Jackson believed this too. He said he would often record his ideas, and if he didn't act on them, they would be passed on to Prince, another famous singer. This reveals an important truth—that God can give you an incredible idea, and how foolish it would be for us to be the only thing standing in the way of its creation and formation.

This is why we must start with ourselves. It is essential to understand your strengths, how you learn and grow, your emotional intelligence, how you interact with others, and how you behave in various situations. You have to walk through the heart work compass to get out your passions, patterns, and purpose. This is essential, and it is challenging. I'm not saying you have to do it all alone or all at once, either. There is a provided roadmap because it is less traveled, so the way forward has to be intentional. Let's face it, eventually your idea will outgrow you, but at that point, it won't be just an idea anymore; it will have taken on a life of its own and grown legs. The question is, will you have the stamina and the fortitude to keep up with it? By truly knowing yourself, you will be able to consistently show up to meet that challenge.

That fully walking idea is still evolving, and it deserves the best version of yourself that you can bring to the table. Much like a baby being developed in the womb deserves a mother who is in the best condition to ensure a smooth and healthy birth for that child. Whatever stressors or blind spots the mother ignores, the baby has to endure. Whatever habits you have been practicing will create ease or discomfort as you try to deliver. Whatever nutrients and healthy atmospheres the mother is positioned in, the child will be groomed and developed in. Is this passion that you want to pursue as important to you as a baby is to an expectant mother? If so, nurse it well and take care of yourself first. It starts with you, and this is the part of the book where you take accountability for your decisions and whatever comes out of you.

Life happens to all of us, and that is understandable; however, today is the day to take inventory of the factors you have added from your personal self that have inhibited your gifts and talents from coming to fruition. Your passions, ideas, plans, and visions deserve a healthy environment in which to grow and flourish. It's all in your hands, both good and bad. If a person is not willing to look at themselves and get dirty first, then there is no reason to continue forward. You have started down an amazing path just by beginning to examine these areas.

If you are reading this and have arrived at this point, you are ready to start a voyage of self-discovery. If you are serious about getting the most out of yourself so that you can light a match to the yearnings within, you have to start with the hard work, which is the heart work. You cannot avoid yourself. Admittedly, I put blood, sweat, and tears partnering with HWork2 to make sure my journey of clarity was clearly laid out for you to follow at your own pace, so you can gain applicable insight into all aspects of who you are in the most comprehensive way.

Scan the QR code below and start the Heart Work Compass: Exploring the Depths of You. Don't half-ass it either because cheating the process is only cheating yourself. Everything inside The HWork2 Method is all about you. It's free, it's simple, and it's as honest as you choose to be. Each question and insight is tailored to help you discover your true self from your own answers. If you don't want to do the hard work, I understand. This is purely for activators, and no one can motivate you to prioritize yourself. I thank you for purchasing this book, supporting me, and taking the time to read the introduction and first chapter.

Perhaps this book would be better gifted to someone else you think is ready to start. But...I have a feeling that you're ready for more. Don't procrastinate and stop here...keep going. We'll meet up again in Chapter 2.

SCAN ME

CHAPTER 02

Potential Is Disgusting

I'm sure that's not how you thought this chapter would start off, but alas, here we are. Here is a phrase that I want you to abandon quickly. "I've got potential." If you are reading this book and have made it this far, I want to declare to you, no matter where you are in the world, that potential is disgusting. Let me address this right away. When I say the word disgusting, I am defining it as something that is extremely unpleasant or unacceptable.

I want you to sit with that statement for a minute before we unpack it, and let's clarify what I am not saying. I am *not* saying that potential is not needed or valuable. After all, it is the secret ingredient in your personal development, serving as the foundation from which your journey begins once your insights are revealed.

Potential is defined as speaking to what is possible and having the capability to develop it into actuality. So that must be the starting point once we lock in and become self-aware. One of the five questions we previously examined in Chapter 1 was: "What do I have?" and that includes your all-encompassing potential.

Remember that it all starts with you. You are the igniter of your passions. You are the captain of your vision. You are the innovator of your idea. You are the person behind your purpose. Scientist Isaac Newton's third law reminds us that consequences don't favor one side over the other; they are simply the by-product of decisions.

However, in all fairness, we must also acknowledge that not every outcome related to your current life situation came with your approval or consideration. Some things just happen. Life has made a mockery of us all in ways that have left us feeling helpless. That comes with playing the cards that we have been dealt, cause life just be lifing. Despite it all, no matter how many times you've been knocked down, you got back up and overcame and still held onto hope. You do have control over your life and what you make of it.

Here is where the disgust reenters the equation. The unpleasant and unacceptable. Simply being okay with potential alone means you've accepted having the capacity without taking any action. Imagine if there were acres of land you owned—space for homes, crops, businesses, entire communities. Yet every day you drive past it, saying, *"This land sure has potential,"* while doing nothing with it. It sounds ridiculous, but that's how many of us treat our own abilities. Even imagining what could be and rewarding yourself for the thought is a form of false progress. Potential only matters when it's activated. You don't get an A in class for Awareness, you get an 'A' for Achievement.

My scenario with the land may seem far off for you if you don't own land, so let me say it more plainly: Potential means nothing without action. Land that's never built on stays empty—just like dreams you never move on.

I want to help you debunk the myth that you are special because you have potential. Everyone has potential; there is nothing inherently unique about skills, capabilities, or talents since we all possess them. They may vary in possession and expression, but we all have these qualities. If they sit dormant, untapped, disengaged, and muted but you still have them, then what good are they and to whom? Inactive potential acts as a daily reminder on the conscious walls of your being of all that you are not doing or have not become, considering your reality. It's the daunting reminder that you have the mental strength, the necessary skillset, the unique position to create the best life for yourself, yet nothing has come to fruition.

So, let's refer to the actual term we are discussing now, which is **unrealized potential**. This term encompasses all the untapped opportunities and possibilities that arise from the skills and talents you possess. All of that capacity to create needs to be utilized or brought to fruition, yet it remains dormant. This is the kind that I refer to as disgusting because you know it's there, and still the problem persists. I get it, and it's different for everyone as to why it's happening, whether it's a lack of confidence, fear, being out of touch with who you are, or simply a lack of available resources. Nonetheless, this is incredibly dangerous because unrealized potential can lull you into a psychosis where you feel like you're in the sunken place.

Unrealized potential can show itself anywhere, and I'll provide a few specific environments:

- **Creatively:** You may have that creative gene or the nature of being organically artistic in your own special way. Perhaps you bring things to life in a meaningful way but settling for just knowing you are a creative can often leave you with an untapped artistic reservoir. Unfinished pieces and unreleased musings that were never able to be appreciated by outside eyes and ears.

- **Intellectually:** If you are an intellectual with special capabilities or a "wiz" like the elders call it, who understands complex things relatively easily, this is a gift. Everyone doesn't think like you, so be patient with others. However, being in this position and not fully applying yourself or underachieving willingly (often in order to fit in) is choosing to feed that disgusting nature over again.

- **Leadership:** Some are natural-born leaders, and it shows in every setting. You have the leadership abilities and qualities to guide and influence people in any space you step into. You can come off as pleasant and still exude authority effortlessly to produce results. Yet, you may choose to shy away from embracing new challenges or taking on responsibilities that help you shine in that area to avoid having the spotlight put on your leadership potential.

Wherever you land, please don't permit yourself to rest in the comfort zone saying you know what you have while doing nothing with it. That may lead to other outcomes that won't serve your whole person in the long run. I've experienced some of these firsthand, and perhaps you can relate.

The pressure and weight that comes with knowing you have what it takes but you aren't where you want to be can show itself by way of health implications tied to anxiety or worry and chronic stress. That constant inner battle leaves you with sleepless nights and incomplete thoughts or brain fog. This is how real it gets! A general ignorance of this could appear to be more blissful temporarily, because once you know, and I mean you really know…it weighs on you every time you don't show, and further inhibits your ability to grow!

Several other substantial impacts to consider with unrealized potential could include:

- Mental & Emotional Stress
- Missed opportunities for advancement
- Stagnation or a lack of growth
- Lack of fulfillment and deep regret
- Questioning your value
- Reinforcing negative self-perceptions

A fundamental part of taking care of ourselves is ensuring we don't allow our talents to become our toxins. Self-polluting from the inside out because they were not released in enough time to do what they were designed to do. They slowly erode and expire, beginning to poison every fabric of our being. If we can see it and feel it, then you must know that your potential and the lack of its activation have an impact on others just as much as it does on you. Flowers and mold can grow from the same foundation.

The Planning Procrastinating Perfectionist

WHEN YOU HAVE POTENTIAL → **BUT NEVER ACT ON IT**

Potential seen by others can weigh heavily on our self-esteem. For the Planning Procrastinating Perfectionist, we often feel anxious because when people notice what we possess, they naturally follow up with questions. Respectfully, they begin to ask about action, timelines, execution, and strategy. Without answers, that once-admired potential quickly feels pitiful. What was once a redeeming quality magnified as grand hope, swiftly turns to a daunting, depressing reminder of your non-movement. And if you're highly skilled with a rare gift (whether musical talent, intellect, physical, or oratory skill), your potential will likely be coveted, yet also scrutinized by a marketplace hungry for innovation.

Here's the truth: those who see you as a shining star or even a golden ticket are eager to invest in you. But upon realizing your mindset and dedication fail to match up to the promise of your potential, they will reposition themselves. The responses you'll face and are about to read are not just possible, they're highly likely, so let's see if these ring a bell.

Impersonation

There will be others who sense your potential and can smell it from a mile away, like a rabid dog with a scent. If they are not gifted in your areas, they may try to befriend you and work alongside you. Be very careful flirting with others from a part of your gifted realm where you have no intention of reviving it. If you are still in the planning and procrastinating phase of perfectionism, it might be better to keep your thoughts to yourself until you're ready for action and watch the company you keep.

What if the potential everyone is coming around you for really is raw greatness? People don't always have the best motives or intentions to help you reach your goals, and sometimes those intentions can be masked by friendship, mentorship, or management. They will maneuver around you to pick up on your patterns, habits, movements, and original content. You may start to notice a lot of new "friends" who have more questions about how you got to where you are and all your processes. Keep in mind that you haven't put out a single thing yet, but they are heavily invested in you, not for the sake of your prosperity, but so they can copy and duplicate your potential for their own success.

You may be asking: *"Why would anyone want to be me, when I'm stuck myself?"*

Here are three reasons why others would choose to impersonate you:

1. **It's a great investment**

   Low-Risk, High Reward is the name of the game, and it's far safer to mimic what has not yet been modeled. By impersonating your style, ideas, and essence, there's less of a chance they can be caught for stealing your intellectual property and branding because you haven't put it out. Even more though, they don't have to outdo the main competition, which is you because you never actually started, so now they look like trailblazers. That's a winning investment with little to no risk in most cases.

2. **Concealed Envy**

   A person will imitate you out of pure projection and dissatisfaction with where they are in life. Instead of creating a life for themselves, seeing all that you could be, they simply recreate yours. The author Oscar Wilde says, "Imitation is the sincerest form of flattery," but in my opinion, it's the lowest form when done out of envy. Without ever reaching their own upper limit, they silence their envy by subtly stealing pieces of your person that they admire most. Sometimes, tragically, they've avoided themselves so much they may not even be consciously aware they are doing it, but it still places you in a position of being impersonated.

3. **Borrowed Light & Leverage**

   You are a shining star, and those with potential often have a certain magnetism that attracts others to them naturally. For those seeking to impersonate you, they may not want to be in your skin, but borrowing your shine and using it as social leverage is enough for them to create a new persona. Understand that an impersonator is someone who is pretending to be someone else. What do they gain here? By staying close to you, they gain the aura that you emit just by association and may even gain credibility in social circles by promising on your potential to others, though you have not yet delivered. This kind of impersonation can feel exploitative and often like someone is feeding off your energy.

Impersonators are everywhere. There's a term for it, and it's called identity theft. People will often be drawn to those like you with potential, since you haven't fully tapped into it. They are not all there to help you grow, but to feed off what's left unused. Think about it: unrealized potential still shines, but it doesn't threaten, while actualized potential demands respect and defines a clear occupied position, which in turn makes you competition. You owe it to yourself to be seen and heard for all that you are before allowing someone else to make it big off of who you naturally were created to be.

Avoidance or Removal

There are those who will notice the things inside of you and can truly see the depths of your capabilities that are impossible to miss. Yet, due to your inactivity, they will abandon any attempt to assist you. Think about this for a moment. In their minds, they saw your potential as a sure thing, and they already positioned themselves to help you get to where they think your talent can take you. They see great things in your future and want to help you get there. Some even have the access, resources, and network to help you live your best life, in their estimation.

When they discover your indifference towards making things happen for yourself after they have created a roadmap of your success in their minds, a shift will take place. That sweet aroma that greeted them every time they saw your image and likeness is replaced with a repudiating stench that they must get as far away from as possible. This is not all on you because you are not responsible for the images of success others project onto you. Whatever they think about your life is their business and not yours to carry. In most of these cases though, we have let people around us into the place where our greatness is found and even shared it with them.

Think about your closest friends and family getting to this point of intolerance with you finally, after years of watching you not bet on yourself. Sure, they won't leave us altogether, but they may distance themselves from discussions about your abilities. You know how it is when you keep giving that one friend advice, and they say they hear you, yet they never apply it in real time or change after the conversation. After a while, we find other things to talk about to keep the relationship progressing. Your potential becomes like that. It becomes common knowledge that we all know, but since you aren't going to do anything anyway, there is no use in talking about it. Instead, loved ones attempt to keep conflict relatively low by navigating around or avoiding this problem area and, in exchange, find other ways to show up for you. Is that what you want? People tiptoeing around the person who never peaked.

Aside from the family and close friends, some people are high-energy and powerhouses. They truly mean well for you from the onset. They are ready to help you take things to the next level, but your lackluster attitude about your own future will drive them away. This process can happen quickly if they don't possess your skills and abilities, or if they covet them in a way that makes them feel intimidated by being in your presence. They may not have leaned into impersonating you like above, but they are on the brink of abandoning you due to frustration. It's not fair, and it's unfortunate to hear, but these are the disgusting consequences that reveal themselves.

You may start to hear phrases like:

- "What a waste of talent."
- "All that, and they don't know what to do with it."
- "It's a shame they don't want more for themselves."
- "If I could do what you do I would be…"
- "I can't be around people who settle."

Take the meat and spit out the bones here, my friend. I know those kinds of phrases evoke feelings within us all, but this is a moment to exercise the muscle of reflection. If the closest people to you have given up on pushing you forward, it isn't always because they don't believe in you. In fact, they are likely rooting for you even still; it's just they can't do the work for you. That doesn't mean your potential is gone, even though they've stopped trying to pull it out of you; it's just that it is yours alone to claim. In many ways, they love you and have given you agency over your own destiny. Now we come to a full circle moment here, again – we can't ignore that hard work. It's time to go back to ask yourself the tough questions because, remember, it all starts with you.

In this, I want you to take comfort because your starting point is not out there, it's in here. The responsibility to act has now shifted back onto you, where it belongs. What's the good news here? As much as their words, disappointment, or abandonment may hurt for a time, you also don't need their permission, applause, or reminders to begin. Prove it to yourself first, even if that means taking a small step, by saying, "I give myself permission to…" This will jumpstart you into action. Until you take full ownership and decide you're done disappointing yourself more than others, people will naturally reposition themselves. Let's act accordingly and attempt not to shift the blame onto others, but to take responsibility for our own way forward.

Come Work With (For) Me

This last one is an environment with which I am very familiar, and I kick myself each time I think about it. So here you are with all your potential talent/skills/ideas, and it is attracting all types of attention. You are noticed by those who genuinely want to help, those who get burned out by your inaction, those who want to be you, and then those who want to use you. All that your reserved gifts and talents need now is a system or an environment that knows how to bring out what you have for the benefit of its own productivity. If you are a dam of water filled with potential, a person needs only to be skilled at piping and running water lines to slowly release everything over time. An untapped supply makes for great turn in profits.

There are those who are not evil or malicious, yet who are uniquely skilled at extracting the best parts of a person within themselves and making it work for the greater good. I know this because not only have I been a person of potential that was used by others, but I am now an extractor of that same potential. The difference is I don't want you to come work for me unless you have something to contribute, and that's your personal choice. I want you to finally work for YOU. That's what this whole book is about, literally getting yourself out of the way to flow freely in your passion. Your potential is disgusting and most likely will be used against you if you don't tap into it.

In some situations, all the stars align, and you find yourself in the perfect environment for your potential to thrive. You waited to get a job to showcase your ability to communicate effectively, be detail-oriented, and demonstrate leadership and meeting-hosting skills. Your superiors are impressed, you receive your bi-weekly paycheck, and everyone is satisfied. The atmosphere of fluorescent lights, 30-minute lunch breaks, hierarchical leadership, and inexpensive office supplies was just enough to bring out all that potential in you.

Consider this: you could have achieved a great deal for yourself on your own, utilizing your potential. However, instead, you traded it for a job that offers a paycheck and a semblance of security. Now, the job that barely pays your bills gets the best of you and your true self, and your goals and passions just gets the rest of you. I know you have seen the quote floating around, "Live your dreams or spend your life building someone else's." That is completely true. This is the way the world works in a capitalist society, and workers are always in demand. Are you comfortable surrendering your deepest treasures to be a worker for someone else while they mind diamonds out of your dirt?

I've spent some time discussing how working for/with someone else is a common response to those with unactualized potential, and that is not inherently wrong. I would not want you to take away that it is not the best path to have or start at a job. After all, this may be the starting launchpad for many of you. I've found myself working corporate 9-5 jobs, and due to the discipline, metrics, focus, and structured environment, it forced my mind to be more accountable and adopt better habits. Naturally, as time went on though my thoughts began to focus on what I truly wanted out of my life while at work, and my hands started to build it. This is where the nuance in these responses lies, and an expansive opportunity for growth.

All the work with (for) me responses aren't malicious. Alternative cases may simply be out of convenience or ease. You may be the person who helps a family member or relative with that task they should pay a professional for, but you do it for free because you are so good at it. You never do it for yourself or even think to monetize it, but for them, you are Johnny on the spot. All those skills you have, cutting and styling hair, you have friends coming over and telling you that you can practice on them. Perhaps you have exceptional skills in administration, and your local non-profit has asked you to volunteer your gift to them in the form of service. There is nothing wrong with serving in that capacity, especially if it's your desire, but when will you launch out into the field of your dreams and stop being pimped by your potential from family, friends, and foes?

I say foes because the side that we don't often see immediately is covertly more harmful. If it's not the environment itself, it could be the person who tells you to come work for them, who also happens to be an opportunist. These sharks are drawn to unrealized potential because it gives them the power to have you by their side and on their team. They may not be impersonating you; they are utilizing you for their own advancement, with your permission. What makes them opportunists and threats is that their alignment with you is primarily driven by control and power dynamics. They can isolate, extract, replicate, and monetize every unique aspect of you at a high level, often for financial gain, while ensuring you remain dormant, which protects their competitive advantage.

This reminds me of the stories of some of our deeply talented black singers and musicians in America, who stood in front of record companies full of White executives salivating over their musical capabilities, that would then offer these artists free recording time. The recording studio, live band, and record were enough for some of the world's greatest talents to relinquish rights, publishing, autonomy, and more royalty money and independence to record companies. They thought they worked *with* a company, but the whole time they worked *for* one. Their talent was likely noticed at some hole-in-the-wall, as they were offered one thing upfront, and they took it immediately. People have created generational wealth on the backs of those who didn't see the value in their potential, while others did. History is our greatest teacher, so take its lessons to avoid becoming one of those people.

It's essential to recognize how quickly things evolve and how rapidly new talent emerges, only to be replaced by something new, allowing for change to occur rapidly and unexpectedly. So, whatever the motives of these environments are (which we may not initially know), try not to get too comfortable here. Although you have what it takes for this to be a great pairing, these individuals and organizations may still feel inclined at some point to return to the former step of repositioning themselves through separation and removal. Your potential is dangerous even to the security of a place you are comfortable at if not used and actualized.

At the base level, I want you to consider that opportunists will always hover, looking to take whatever they can. But if even they decide to walk away because of your indifference and inaction, that shift speaks louder than words. When someone who thrives on taking your value for their own benefit can't find anything else to use, it means your potential has gone cold. In my sales experience, they'd call it a dead lead. In life, it's worse as it means even your wasted potential no longer looks like an opportunity.

Potential is Disgusting

Hear me clearly, it is not a problem if someone sees your potential and highlights it. You should just be careful with flaunting it around like the main character without action accompanying it.

 Your belief in your potential alone is enough to keep you paralyzed. A paralytic filled with great promise is what becomes of a person who only dreams about the talents and skills they possess, yet never acts on them. Life is filled with deep regret, resentment, unmet expectations, bitterness, and ultimately a loss of hope. But you still have time to choose something different. Remember the saying that dreams become goals when they have a deadline. What will you build out of the developing arena of your potential, and when can we expect it?

I was scrolling online one day and I saw a gripping image that took my breath and tied this all together so beautifully. I couldn't grasp why I was unable to look away from the picture and why it had such a profound effect on me. Feelings that rushed to me so clearly as I felt – Connected. Seen. Disappointed. Hopeful. It was this abandoned house that invoked those feelings:

This image was gripping me and so I scoured the internet for the source until I discovered it in an online group called "Abandoned Mansions." It also revealed the location where this was as an abandoned row home located in Philadelphia, my home city. It made sense now as to why it evoked so much emotion and led to a connection from within; I grew up my whole life passing homes that looked like this, and I've watched them go through full life cycles in totally different states. This was a very familiar and consistent setting for me.

From this image, I began to ponder deeply as I looked at the domicile. I started to infer what could have happened to this corner property, and the first thing I asked was, "Where is the rest of the house?" If this is a row home and there is a lot next to it, that suggests the home next door may have been destroyed or demolished, leaving only a grass patch. Was there

a fire, or was it removed due to major architectural or structural damage?

Then I looked more closely, and I began to examine the house that remained. It felt incomplete. I had seen houses like this that were in great condition and shone bright as corner properties despite being vacant. They often had a thriving porch, restored or original bricks, window dressing, good landscaping – but not this house. What was the story of this house? Could it ever regain its former glory or reveal something even greater later? Naturally, I'll be honest, my mind did not go to the initial thought of wondering what the house used to look like, because the way I am wired, I immediately went to the potential of thinking about what it could be if the homeowner had taken some initiative to bring this house to life. We can't go backwards in life and think about what could have been and what once was. We must work in the here and now, focusing on potential in the present, with a plan for construction that will yield a finished product for the future. So, I became even more intrigued, and when I visited the page to look at homes like this, my eyes darted to several others. Ironically, I was drawn to the ones from my home state.

I looked at the familiar and empathized with these homes. I had been in similar houses like this, and I knew the possibilities of their full development. This drew a point up for me. Often, we look at a situation or person and are disappointed with their approach, while attempting to suggest what should be done instead. Isn't it amazing how easily we can project onto others what we would do in their situation or with their possessions, but we forfeit acting on what's right in front of us?

The message that spoke to me quite clearly here was: **Get your house in order!** Stop driving around the neighborhood talking about others when you haven't even owned your own shit! Draw up your own blueprints before envisioning someone else's. Keep your porch swept before you complain about their unkept landscaping. At the same time, don't gasp and marvel at everything that is around you being built up while feeling bad about yourself. We are all living the human experience. So, work with what you have, where you are, at this very moment.

For every single one of us who is sitting idle on our potential, we are an eyesore of abandoned houses to a world of passing-by strangers. Strangers who are looking for somewhere to dwell. How would anyone know to look through the rubble when the outside showed disregard and vacancy? Do not be an abandoned house of urban blight until one day you're demolished, cleared, and turned into a grassy field. Tricking yourself out of your own spot for a new ambitious developer to come build on the land you once owned is crazy work, and yet it happens every day!

There is more in store for you, my friend, and there is **life within**.

CHAPTER 03

The Theory of Moore

"Life will meet you at your level of audacity."
—Case Kenny

There is a scene in the 2010 movie "Wall Street: Money Never Sleeps" that has forever stuck with me as one of the most powerful mindset moments I've witnessed on a big screen. This young and ambitious Wall Street trader, played by Shia LaBeouf, is newly hired to work at a hedge fund, and he asks the seasoned executive Bretton James, played by Josh Brolin, a profound question. "What's your number? The amount of money you would need to just walk away from it all and live?"

He goes on to say, "You see, I often find that everybody has a number and it's usually an exact number, so what's yours?" Brolin looks away, attempting to hold back a slight smirk, shakes his head swiftly, and, with a grin, looks up at this young man with a sense of pride. The background movie score starts rising with the strings of the orchestra as he looks at Shia LaBeouf with a twitch of his head and says, **"More."** He turns around and smiles as he exits the room.

For me, there is something about an individual who is always hungry but doesn't have a number or a ceiling for growth that just gets me amped! "More" was his number. Of course, it highlights the greed of hedge fund owners on Wall Street, but the concept and mindset that their abundance is limitless is what I took away from it, and that brings us to the substance of this chapter.

The Theory of Moore

When I discovered I could use my last name for all types of cool things like to show increase and abundance, I nearly lunged at it. Moore. All my endeavors fall under the mantra of M4M – *Made 4 Moore* as the flagship of my beliefs and life's mission no matter what the endeavor. It's a declaration and a constant reminder that I am made for more! In my young-adult years, when I published my third hip-hop album and first solo project, it was called "There's Moore." In the next era of my life, when I tried my hand at blogging, I created "Moore Thoughts." I thoroughly enjoy the play on words as a distinct identifier, while also attributing my works to things related to a desire for continual elevation that has not yet been fully realized.

Every single human being on this earth was made to experience more than what they currently are in this present moment: more joy, more love, more success, more challenges, more peace, more territory, more increase, more advancement. In addition, I believe that the more you produce from a weak position, the more you gain to strengthen you. This is the **Theory of Moore**.

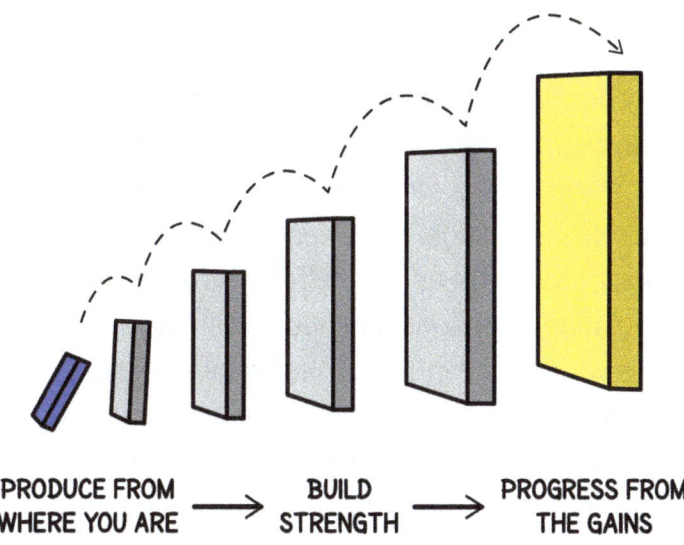

Dive In

We are unique and advanced human beings with the immense capability, despite our vices and fears, to produce greatness in every facet of life—fashioned in the likeness of something that is ethereal, yet complex. This earth is ours for the taking of natural expansion and dominion. Not to make one another subservient but to rule together in abundance, with responsibility, unto great increase and multiple dimensions of wealth and prosperity for all. Showcasing dominion through learning from our past toxic traits and patterns that limited our fullest potential from evolving. Humanity is here to continue evolving and discovering, as we innovate to make space for future generations. This is why we must allow our creativity to flourish.

Taking it to the grave with you robs the ones after you, and that charts an entirely different legacy left behind.

So, what I'm saying is to stop settling! It's not enough for us to endure Monday through Friday in a job we hate and live for happy hour and the weekends. That modality is inherently flawed and supremely limiting. We wait for several hours of happiness and for our week to come to an end, seeking rest, comfort, release, solace, and peace. Programming is draining and, in turn, has made us less fulfilled. We numb ourselves by overstimulating our brains and bodies with agents to convince ourselves we are unwinding when we are only furthering the distance from reconnecting with our inner selves. This has confined our creativity while snuffing out the possibility of living in and on purpose in the time that we do have.

The number of people in loveless relationships or unforgiving families continues to grow. You deserve more. We often pursue achievements and degrees to satisfy societal expectations instead of following our own passions. You deserve more. We cling to friendships that have long since expired, holding onto them for the sake of history rather than seeking wholeness and reciprocity. You deserve more. Rules, policies, and judgments placed on us were merely inherited and never questioned until their flaws were exposed—showing they did not benefit us all equally. You deserve more.

The Theory of Moore needs to exist for you. The truth behind that is that you deserve all that you seek if you are willing to put in the work and dive into the deep end of your fears. Your fear is not going away; it is neces-

> **You were made for more!**

sary to keep you level and help you navigate trouble. How long will you stand on the edge of the deep end, telling all your neighbors you have a pool, but you're scared to swim in it yourself? I love the analogy of a large body of water because, though we are not aquatic creatures by nature, even as land mammals, there is beauty under the sea. In the water, we feel different, we exist differently, there are different rules, our bodies regulate differently, and our movement itself is harder yet rewarding work! The fear of drowning underwater without oxygen is only more looming because there is no equal threat in breathing on earth while never earnestly living. On solid ground, you don't feel suffocating pressures around you forcing you to fight for your life, and so you breathe easily here without a care. We take for granted what we have been given freely until it's not available, then we panic.

Learn how to swim in the terrifying waves of your greatest desires. Let's go back to the analogy. It's not enough to tell people that you have a pool, and you just put your feet in from time to time. For a person like this, who is either fearful of water, never learned to swim, or simply content with owning a luxury they don't use, such as a beautiful in-ground pool, there is a lot forfeited. Imagine all the opportunities you have passed up on, vacations with sea activities or aquatic amenities. Think about the experiences that a cruise provides that your fear of water has kept you from. The limitless exploration that can be found in deep sea scuba diving, parasailing, jet skiing, or snorkeling. What about the joy from feeling the cool rush hit you at a water theme park as you take it all in under the radiant sun? How many more opportunities have you squandered by not maximizing your life experiences due to fearing the water and its depths?

The more you produce right now from a weak position, the more you will gain back to be strengthened. I know that your plan is airtight and rock-solid because you've been rehearsing it for a long time. Do you know how many notebooks, pads, digital notes, and Word documents I've had over the years with the same themed plans jotted down in them? And absolutely no work done until right now. I am the king of plans. Have you ever felt like that? You are so organized and efficient that you have everything written down and planned out, and yet still no results?

What is your excuse? I can tell you why I procrastinated for so long — it was because I had other responsibilities that I thought were more important. My career, relationships, family outings, leisure activities, commitment to others' causes, etc. While all good things, they somehow added to my need to procrastinate. I had no idea that I needed to prioritize the deepest longings of my heart over the things that I was doing for the sake of comfort or routine. Here's why – oftentimes our deepest passions, ideas, and desires are not going to meet our immediate needs. Let's be honest. Your devotion to the thing you have been fostering will not immediately pay your bills. It will cost you more upfront, it takes tremendous amounts of time, it won't make sense to those closest to you, and it's entirely too risky. So, you procrastinate and come up with real "adult" reasons as to why you aren't living fully. Procrastinating in this step is detrimental because it justifies postponing what you ought to do now and calls your plans an act of achievement. It's always easier to procrastinate after you have a plan because at least you have a plan. I know it's true because we all do it or are currently doing it.

If you are charged up enough to compile your plans, lucky enough not to delay it with procrastination, then your final hurdle awaits you – perfectionism. Remember, the more you produce right now from a weak position, the more you will gain back to be strengthened.

That brings up a thought from my middle school years. I'm from a generation that saw the emergence of the internet, and prior to it, my father bought me a typewriter for Christmas. I was intrigued but hated it at the same time because each time I made a spelling error while typing on those keys, I ruined the whole document. As frustrating as it was to load up a new sheet of paper or release the paper in the tray, white it out, load it back up, and continue typing – I did it! There was a valuable lesson to be learned in that it taught me great patience. And even then, it still wouldn't be perfect.

Perfectionism takes up too much time that you are not owed and robs you of your true self. There are things that you will be able to do when you are younger that will be more difficult at an older age, if not impossible. The innovation that you may have had in one season may be outdated and exploited by the time you are finished perfecting it in your mind. Some of you are single and may be able to accomplish more before entering a committed relationship and having children, in some cases. Your perfectionism has you living with less while the imperfect self-starters are taking more. This is a very difficult habit to break because you care for your creation and want to nurse it to being fully mature. Some of us have been feeding our ideas breast milk for too long, so now it's time for solid food. The next stage of your development requires that you trust that everything won't go as you planned, no matter how long you wait and how much you try.

The weak position you are in will yield strong results if you simply start where you are and with what you have. Put your wants to the side for a second and realign your priorities to focus on your needs – and for these three, you don't need anyone's permission to take hold of them. Consistency, Focus, and Discipline. That's it.

Whatever you are currently experiencing, even if it is *seemingly* a place of greatness and abundance, there is more. You'd better know it. If you've finally made your vision board and feel accomplished, congratulations! However, there are a host of other initiatives waiting for you that will exponentially match the dopamine rush you received from that small win. Celebrate your small victories and wins, and keep moving to the more. There is an opportunity awaiting anyone who has the audacity and willingness to chase it relentlessly, at all costs, and knows it is theirs for the taking. This requires vision to see. Without a vision, though you exist, you are already dead – you are just blind to it.

Move Like It's Yours

In 2013, the world watched and created a comical meme of Kanye West on *the Sway in the Morning* radio show, where he ranted about the fashion industry and his frustrations and hurdles in overcoming certain challenges. The infamous rant of "You don't have the answers, Sway" turned into a global comedic strip and viral quote for years. Fast forward to 2021, at his peak, Kanye became a billionaire, worth $6.6 billion, and the highest-grossing rapper with his YEEZY brand, with sole ownership and had partnered with Gap and Adidas. Over the next several years, the road got rough for Kanye between his mental health, his relationship with his ex-wife, and ultimately a severing of ties with Adidas. Yet, my point here is to focus on his accomplishments.

Kanye knew he was worth more than what the fashion industry was telling him, and despite all the blockades and criticism, he surpassed even Jay-Z in net worth and has a retail success story that took less than eight years to grow, with shoes that rival Michael Jordan's in popularity. Kanye took a step and may have even looked crazy while doing it, but that makes room for people like Pharrell Williams, who became the Men's Fashion

Creative Director at Louis Vuitton's in 2023 after the passing of the iconic Virgil Abloh. Someone must be crazy enough to believe it will work to knock down the invisible door and shatter the glass ceiling, so that the rest of us can know itis okay to want to be more than just a rapper, actor, or athlete.

This is the part where you start to compare your success to that of celebrities and Google their net worth. Naturally, you are looking for an excuse cloaked as a relevant reason as to why this can't happen for you. Your brain works to conceptualize the examples I'm saying and simplify them so you can feel better. Neuroplasticity works that way, which is why I keep interrupting this book with some of your intrusive thoughts to cause you to start understanding yourself. It's easy to look at the aforementioned persons and say, "Well, they have more money than I, so it's no wonder they are successful."

Is more money the problem/answer?

Under the Theory of Moore, I discovered something that allowed me to embrace who I was even more and release the false equivalency that money equals success. The simple notion that:

Money is Not Real

Take a moment to soak it in and let it sink in. In the year 2020, through the global pandemic and COVID-19, in over three months, the Federal Reserve printed three trillion dollars' worth of money to add into the economy. Out of thin air, they turned on their printing presses and flushed the economy with fresh new currency. How does a nation do that if money is so real?

Let's have a quick economics lesson. The U.S. Dollar was once backed by gold that could be internationally owned and used for trade. Known as "the gold standard," international currencies and paper money found their value in the nation's gold. Despite the world's best attempts from 1879 to 1933, the gold standard proved too volatile and lacked the stability necessary to keep pace with a growing population, ultimately failing. After the Great Depression in 1933, President Franklin D. Roosevelt coordinated policies to move the U.S. away from the international gold standard. In 1971, President Nixon effectively severed the connection between gold and currency due to inflation and introduced a new term: Fiat Money.

Fiat money is quite funny to me because it reminds me of Monopoly. The word "Fiat" is Latin, which translates as 'Let it be done', and the word fiat in usage is a binding edict issued by a person in command. So, the only thing backing the U.S. Dollar in place of a physical commodity like gold or silver is the people's faith and trust in the government that issued it. That same government delegates its powers to its nation's central bank, which is known as the Federal Reserve (The Fed), to oversee the entire monetary system of the nation. They are independent of the government and yet are held accountable in part by Congress. This is why every piece of U.S. currency is marked as a 'Federal Reserve note.' It's simply a piece of paper that we all collectively agree on has value because we put our trust in the government. The government appoints a separate autonomous entity (The Fed), which explains its actions in layman's terms, essentially saying, "trust us." Now you see, if you have the people's trust and faith, then it's easy to print three trillion dollars and flood it into an economy during 2020 for the pandemic, while no one bats an eye.

Let's Talk Money!

Money is not real; it is a tool. Tools are devices that are used to carry out and implement tasks. What's remarkable is that many people will skip starting with themselves and jump right to wanting to make money. They haven't checked their self-inventory or done any heart work. Instead, they believe that if I have the right tools, they can complete the job. Just because you have the tools doesn't mean you have the discipline, the drive, the knowledge, the ambition, or the relentlessness to see it through.

You want to make money, manage money, and move money. Ask yourself a more valid question: before the money, have you been making changes? Have you been managing your habits and disciplines? Have you been moving in a way that shows consistency and determination? Have you been doing more?

> ***Many people want dollars,***
> ***but what they first need is change.***

You may have been blaming money for a long time for why you haven't done a thing and neglected to do more as a result. It's interesting how we make money, the motivator, the problem, and the solution all in one. The story repeats itself over and over in your mind until you've become indoctrinated to believe it.

- "The problem is I don't have enough money to get started. If I had the money, I could…"
- "I would be more motivated if I had the money to accomplish my goals and get this off the ground."
- "Once I start and this is finally taking off, I know this is going to make me so much money!"

Money is not the end-all, be-all because it is not real; therefore, stop blaming it. I invite you to challenge yourself for a moment to think differently. Money can't buy you the joy, the peace, the happiness, or the sense of fulfillment you seek. Those who are wealthy will tell you that they suffer from loneliness and feel empty despite their money. Others in higher tax brackets will assure you that it's easier to have less because, like the famous rapper Notorious B.I.G. once said, "More money, more problems." You and I may think that those statements are easier said from a place of wealth, but let's examine what money really does, because I believe we seldom think about what it affords us.

Money provides three things:

1. Access
2. Networks
3. Resource

MONEY'S KEY PURPOSE…

…IS TO OPEN DOORS

ACCESS   NETWORK   RESOURCE

I have found that people largely want money for those three things above. It's not the currency in our pocket that we want; it's the ability to gain access, have the right network, and secure the resources that money provides. We use money as a means to secure what we perceive as assets. That's it. Many of us have idolized a federal reserve note that is not backed by any real value, and we chase it without realizing we are only in pursuit of what it provides, not what it is. The person who has the resources, networks, and access has the power and unlocks new levels of freedom. That is the same thing that money can provide.

Ask yourself this question: What if I could get all the things money provides before or without actually possessing the money?

1. Access

The access that you are looking for is to different places and spaces that you didn't have the privilege to enter before because you were not deemed by society as "qualified." Money can grant you access, however, so can the execution of your genius. Your action and consistency qualify you and will gain you access to places of privilege before you even get paid! Here is a quick note for you to jot down: **exposure leads to experience, which gives you new expectations!** I have watched those who have remained teachable and become mentees or apprentices get the same access as millionaires simply because they were available and willing to do the work. They didn't overthink it, they understood their insights, and they didn't underrate themselves. They just showed up and knew they wanted more, and voilà – access granted.

Quit chaining your success and your "more" to money and focus on what you truly want. You want the access. If you put your work first and your passion in front of you to showcase how skilled you are, then the backstage passes come easy because you belong there. If you have a seat at the table, it's not because you bought a ticket; it's because you brought an appetite and you are ready to eat. Actualized potential. You are the asset, and it's an honor to have you dine with us. Flip your thinking and break this, and watch access be the real door you've been searching for.

A while ago, a question floated that had the culture divided: if you had to choose, would you take dinner with Jay-Z or $500,000? People were torn between the two and had a myriad of reasons for both. If given $500k with their current mindsets, most people wouldn't even know what to do with it. I remember Jay answered the question in an interview later on and said he would tell people to take the money, but what he said afterwards was the real takeaway. He said, "Take the money because I've already laid out the blueprint in my music of how I did what I do, just go buy the records." His music and lyrics already gave us access to hard lessons and core truths. That's powerful…some of us only moved to the beat and missed the blueprint. For me, however, I would take the dinner because if compelled enough to sit with me individually over a meal and share wisdom, I know that's all I would need to get into the network, and that is, as they say, "where the money resides."

2. Network

It's funny how people repeat this popular phrase "your network is your net worth" and live in opposition to it. If you still have money on the pedestal and done nothing to enhance your network you will remain broke. With the wrong people around you even with money it won't last long. This is why as we elevate so do our relationships, it's just a natural progression. If I'm hungry for more, I need people with the same level of hunger to match my energy and keep me driven and accountable. Highlight this misconception here: people often think "having money brings me around those with money." That may be true in part, but are they the right people? All money isn't good money, and that goes for the ones tied to it. What's the point of being invited to a private island because I'm wealthy, but it's owned by Jeffrey Epstein? So, having money doesn't mean they will be aligned with your best interests, or that they align with your character and mission.

A strong network is the lifeblood of legacy and continued growth. We grow from one another and enrich each other. In the Theory of Moore, I explained how it's about ruling together and setting up the next generation, not dominating one another but conquering uncharted territories together. Money doesn't create risk takers; struggle does. The more you produce from a weak position, the more you gain back to strengthen you. This is reflected in the ideology of "getting it out of the mud" or "day ones," referring to people who have been battling alongside you in the trenches. Those people who believed in your dreams and invested, showed up, and helped you iron out those details. If you're lucky, they will remain to become your trusted confidants and network when you elevate. Your network ranges from those who took risks with you when there was no money in sight, expanding to those who know what it's like to bet it all on their goals.

All good business is built on good relationships. If you can't build relationships and communicate with people, you won't get far in business. Strong networks will amplify and multiply your money ten times over. This is the real end goal when we say we want or need money; we actually need a solid network. That is the security blanket of a village that will always hold you down and expose you to new opportunities and ventures, and perhaps give you more of the first item, which is access. I hope one day that you will be part of mine after you complete this book.

3. Resource

It's a fact that money provides resources, and there is no getting around it. The fastest way to acquire a commodity or an asset is to buy it. Let's dive into the alternative ways though. What if I didn't have money? How would I acquire resources? This ties back to everything we have discussed up to this point. If I start with myself and do the hard work, which is the heart work, I will sharpen my character, self-awareness, and communication, and ultimately, how I show up in the world with these new insights. By doing so, I will be able to recognize my potential and activate it, rather than allowing it to remain dormant. This follows from attracting the right people and developing the right relationships that will help me build a new network, giving me access to valuable resources.

Resource is defined as a useful or valuable possession of available supply or support. The word originates from Latin and French, as the word root evolved from a Latin verb to a French noun, retaining the same core meaning. The root is the Latin verb:

Re – meaning "again"
Surgere – meaning "to lift up" or "to rise"

These two words sound a lot like resurge, right? That's because, as a verb, that is exactly what it meant.

The French took it from old to new verbs until it found its way into English in the 1600's as a noun. So Resurgere (to rise again) became resource (to supply and help).

Here is why words matter yet again. A resource is just that – an "again" source. It provides relief, support, and help, which has been made available to almost everyone. Never confuse the two: a Resource is not The Source. So, although you have access to a resource in front of you that can change your entire trajectory, it cannot bring relief to the one without clarity and awareness of their insights. The resource can only go as far as the person because they are the source in question being aided and assisted. Now you don't have to wonder anymore why, despite resources being available to certain communities, they don't benefit from them. It's an abandonment of self-issue, and you can't lift up again what never got up in the first place.

You are an asset, and you must work on maintaining and maturing as such so that you don't become a liability. I've watched millionaires invest in individuals who consistently put in the work in their lane and craft it with excitement, because they couldn't duplicate the discipline and commitment of the person, they chose to invest in. This is how the world works! If you show up and never stop showing up, everything that you think you need money to accomplish on your own first can present itself in a different form. Be open to receiving a resource that may present itself in ways that your ego or old environment would normally reject. This is where you shine when you are focused more on the mission than the money.

The Theory of Moore teaches you a valuable lesson: instead of chasing money, pursue the things it provides and watch the money show up as a result. It has no other option. Money is attached and attracted to those doors. The weak position that you are in will produce strong results if you start where you are with what you have.

It Matters What You Do

When I look at the history of enslaved Africans in the United States who were given so little and were required to do so much, it is fascinating. The amount of work our ancestors had to do in labor would suggest that they should be in optimal health to complete those grueling tasks, but that was not their reality. They were not afforded the luxuries of basic human decency. Instead, their food rations were bare bones of cornmeal, rice, with some pork and maybe a chicken or two. If they were lucky, they would get food on the brink of spoiling. In many cases, they would be required to grow their own vegetables to feed themselves and have just enough to have the strength for a day's work in the sweltering sun. Yet, they made much with the very little they had.

We are fashioned in a way to experience more even when we are given less, if we possess the will to reach for it. Looking at today's menu, the basis of soul food, which has been commercialized and monetized, is rooted in the survival strategies of enslaved people, who often relied on cornmeal, greens, and a local catch of fish or a chicken.

I need you to understand that it doesn't matter what you are given, what matters is what you do with it. The work is still before you, and no matter how hard it is, or how unfair it may seem, or how people down the road may be living in a better condition than you, what you have can be made into more. That is the mindset you must adopt in this Theory of Moore.

I recall being laid off from my first corporate job due to downsizing. The director called me into his office, which had a frosted glass door, and asked me to close it behind me. Bare in mind, this was my first salary-paying job in corporate America. After changing locations with this company three times, being a high earner, and pitching and creating a special position for myself, I was certain they would keep me. After all, I caught two buses both ways for an hour and eleven minutes to get to this job. They needed me, and I gave them all my potential as the perfect people pleaser.

I sat down across from the director and my supervisor with a white envelope on the table. Contrary to most sitcoms, it's not an actual pink slip. They spoke softly, explaining the company's downsizing and how they had to let staff members go. My mind was racing, and I thought this was the end, but I didn't know how to move from the sunken position. They offered me a severance package, extended benefits, and asked if I would like them to cover the cost of a taxi to take me home. I declined. In my pride, I packed up my things and went across the street in my shirt and tie and sat at the bus stop.

I recall mumbling to myself in anger and disappointment wrapped in one as I opened the severance letter and looked at the dollar amount. I took out my cellphone and recorded a video describing what had happened to me that day, declaring that I would make more money on my own in 45 days than I would from this entire severance check. I needed to know in that moment that all my efforts and attempts were worth something. My value and dignity had been shattered, and I refused to be like my friends on unemployment, living at home with their parents, settling for scraps. I knew I was worth more because the job showed me over time what accommodations they were willing to make for me, and now I was out on my ass without a second thought. I bet on them instead of myself. I built their dreams and delayed my own, and when it was time for them to change directions, I was cast aside as collateral damage.

I set out to prove them wrong and make something out of nothing because even then, I knew I was the asset. I recall joining a multi-level marketing company I discovered on YouTube, which was popular at the time, and documenting all the money I earned. I went hard as a natural salesman, driven by deep motivation and the ability to convince people to try anything, in my twenties. I was all over social media and racing through my contacts. I used everything at my disposal and harassed everyone I knew in my network trying something that didn't seem perfect, but it was the vehicle I thought was necessary and I was determined. The hustle was simple, they paid $40 for the program, and I got $80 for referring them and they in turn could do the same. My dignity was on the line and that's all I had. I had to believe that I was worth more than waiting on a job to pay me, and it didn't matter the vehicle I used to get there.

Sure enough, in 45 days I surpassed that severance check amount in earnings. Imagine how much further and for how much longer I would have pushed if I knew that the return on my time and money would mean that my wildest dreams and passions would come true. This is an example of what I accomplished during that time, which showed me that with the right determination and discipline, there is no limit. Although that was short-lived, the lessons I learned and the businesses I started apart from that are still elements I use to this day. I got what I deserved, as a matter of fact, I left with more than I deserved. **This is the Theory of Moore.**

There is a mindset shift that must occur for you to leap into the area of the unknown, where you tap into all that awaits you. First, however, we must tackle the entire reason you picked up this book. The anecdotes, history lessons, allegory, illustrations, developmental tools, potential diving, and theories aren't why you are here. We have to dissect the core issue...

You have been living life in **3P: Planning. Procrastination. Perfectionism.**

This is the elephant in the room that has made a circus of your grand stage while you juggle like the featured clown, attempting to keep up. They say the best way to eat an elephant is one piece at a time, so expect us to chop this down so you can digest what exactly has you stuck in your head. To understand how to adopt a new mindset, let's start with those plans of yours.

CHAPTER 04
The Planning

"Plans are nothing, planning is everything."
—Dwight D. Eisenhower

The planning stage is what we all love the most, isn't it? If you have been fiddling with ideas and aspirations, planning finally takes it to the next level. This stage enables you to gain mental clarity and establish a sense of control by organizing your thoughts into tasks with timelines and tools. All the uncertainty in your mind can be sketched down and controlled within the lines of your plans, and you finally start placing expectations on what is to be accomplished with precision.

Plans prove that you are organized and serious and that what you have is more than a pipe dream. Planning shows you have vision, have evaluated risk, researched strategized, and marked a path to success.

A plan is crucial if you want to achieve success in life, as it outlines a strategic roadmap to reaching your desired destination. We all plan, even subconsciously, but you are reading this book because you don't just plan, you **over plan**. That's right, and you do it nearly every time. You have fail-safes and contingencies set up for the first plan, even if it isn't in motion yet. Like me, I'm sure you have your journal notes, stickies, bookmarks, and examples as you refine this perfect plan repeatedly. You may even go as far as to start planning things that have nothing to do with the initial plan, completely sidetracking you. This why you are stuck procrastinating and not having any fun in your motion.

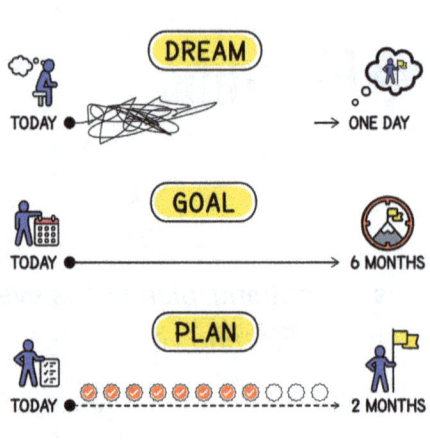

This process sound familiar? The dream is magical when you first have it, and it lifts you off your feet into another realm. As your neurons start firing, you begin connecting real-world dots with your other-world fantasies, and that's when you draw up a plan to make it happen. A plan does not close the gap of making

> **Overplanning kills the magic.**

the impossible possible; only action can do that. Therefore, the logical next step is action – not more planning, just deliberate action. But then your anxiety kicks in and forces you to try to control the uncontrollable of the future so much that you over plan and kill the magic of the present. **The joy is in the journey, while the deliverance is in the destination, but your anxiety has robbed you of both.** My friend, you must suspend yourself from overplanning because you are withdrawing from your person the magic of the moment you so rightfully deserve.

I can recall most of my childhood vacations with my family. My father was a planner and somewhat of a strict household authoritarian. Back when the internet was fresh, in the late 1900's we didn't have GPS navigation in cars or cell phones, so we had to print out MapQuest directions when we traveled. Yes, I'm dating myself here, but add this to my resumé as part of my depth of experience. Prior to each vacation, my younger sister and I would be ecstatic to go on a road trip to the beach or an amusement park, so we would pack our bags in a frenzy. We had hopes of jumping in tidal waves, eating funnel cake, going to the buffets, getting on all the rides two times over, and so much more. The only problem is that we never considered the person who oversaw this vacation to be an over planner.

My father's desire for control and a sense of what he perceived as ease and the "perfect" vacation would set the stage for a very limited experience for the rest of the family, to say the least. He printed the directions out days in advance, mapped the time it would take to get there, and only allowed for minimal restroom stops along the way. Okay, I can somewhat understand that. After all, prioritizing efficiency is the best way to start a good trip. Yet because of his strict nature, the car ride of laughter and loud antics while traveling got stifled as we were coerced into playing the "quiet game" to see which sibling could be quiet the longest. Little did we know that was just a parental trick to get peace of mind from the nagging kids on a long road trip.

When we arrived at the hotel, we were usually hours early, so we had to wait to check in. Upon going out, we had to wear certain clothes, and on the boardwalk, we couldn't stop in every store like we thought. Going down to the beach, we were told we would only be allocated a certain time limit because we had a dinner reservation. Oh, and we could forget about the funnel cake today, since we had to save our appetite. All these plans for a vacation—I just couldn't understand. What happened to the magic of it all? We started out being told we were going to take a trip to Disney World, had two-day passes, and would have the time of our lives. How did we end up attending a timeshare presentation for nearly the entire first day, only to be able to leave to enjoy select rides with the remaining time? Where did the magic go? It was killed and suffocated by the plans and desire to control every single aspect of what was supposed to be an enchanted adventure.

By the end of it all, I was tired of the family vacations. This same feeling occurred for me when we hosted summer family cookouts and our annual Christmas brunch. These family gatherings didn't feel like a time of joy, but rather an event that needed to be perfectly presented, with no room for fun or relaxation, because everything had to go according to plan. (Later, I'll delve more into how these experiences informed some of my own struggles with perfectionism that I had to acknowledge as I grew older and did the necessary heart work.)

You see, overplanning is a form of overthinking. What do we miss out on because of overplanning? What memories were we robbed of by not existing in the moment of the unknown? Was there enjoyment or just enduring? This is one cost of overplanning – it kills the magic. The leaps and bounds we take enjoying the journey as we go are replaced with mental hurdles trying to be the architect of the perfect plan. There is no magic left, just systems and a lack of enjoyment.

The cost of overplanning is never starting at all. You have all the plans and contingencies laid out, and you still never start. You constantly delay the start because you are not fully certain that your plans will work out. This is a crippling paradigm that is created when you get in your own way and allow your mind to overtake your movement. Instead, your ambition should be taking action to ignite your plans. Overplanning in time can lead to natural procrastination, often due to the planning fallacy, as it is impossible to account for every dynamic variable that may change along the way.

Why Are We Like This?

Let's take a moment to address what the planning fallacy is in case you have never heard of it. The **Planning Fallacy** is a type of cognitive bias in which individuals tend to underestimate the amount of time required to complete a future task. This is due in large part to a reliance on overly optimistic performance scenarios that leave no room for error, as they rely on perfection. Why is this dangerous outside of scaring you because your plans are too perfect? It leaves no room for grace, and so when you don't meet the mark or something unexpected hits you, you have less compassion for yourself. Do not underestimate the time and energy required to complete a future task.

"Everyone has a plan...until they get punched in the face."
—Mike Tyson

Most times, your plans are so great to you that you don't mind failing, but you don't want people to see you fail, so you don't perform anything. At a perceived standstill, but more akin to being on a treadmill running closer to your goals because they are the only things in front of you. You feel exhausted and think you're putting in work, but you haven't applied anything in the real world that is worth the risk. Instead of placing practice over planning, you just practice overplanning.

This is all rooted in fear, somewhat like a person who has agoraphobia, an extreme irrational fear and sense of anxiety of being in a public or crowded place, where escaping is more difficult, resulting in some form of a panic attack. As a result, an agoraphobic would much rather stay in their home than deal with public places and the unknown dangers of being unable to escape. Your plans are likened to your house in this instance, and you are petrified of the outside world. It is your fear turned anxiety that has you stuck in your house, surrounded by your sketches and musings. I want to challenge you to be honest with yourself and ask the following questions:

- Do you go back and revise the plans to make them feel fresh again?
- Are you spending hours online comparing your life to everyone else who you perceived started and is further than you?
- Does looking at it makes you second guess yourself and your self-worth?
- Will the plans be so overwhelming and the realization that you haven't started cause you to sink into a depressive state?
- Do you share some of your plans with trusted confidants so they can give you the dopamine rush and ego boost to know you're still amazing even though you haven't done anything?

Maybe you are like me, and you do all five of those things, shuffling back and forth like a mad genius and a scared child all in one. Deliverance is in the destination, but are you willing to start the journey? You may never have viewed yourself as a timid, self-doubting, introverted type. You may view yourself as a confident person who knows their plans will come to fruition. You aren't one to back down from your goals, and you look well accomplished on the outside. Why then are you still in the same position of inactivity as the former person? I was just like you before I discovered what was happening inside that was contrary to what was displayed on the outside.

This behavior prevented me from progressing and often goes undiagnosed because it is masked by movement. This is called **High Functioning Anxiety.** Instead of looking debilitated, retreating from opportunities, or shy and fearful, I was a go-getter who was always saying yes, and showed my prowess and potential. Take a brief look at the differences between generalized anxiety and the often undiagnosed and undefined high-functioning anxiety:

TWO TYPES OF ANXIETY

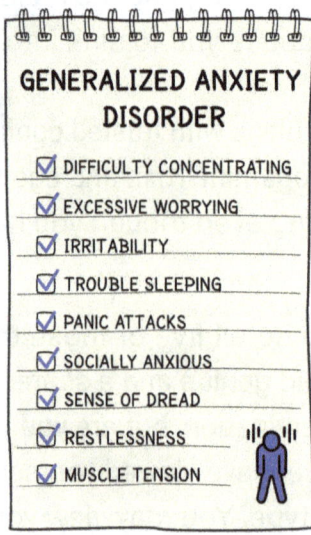
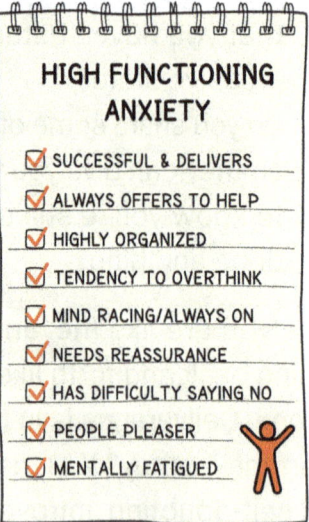

GENERALIZED ANXIETY DISORDER	HIGH FUNCTIONING ANXIETY
☑ DIFFICULTY CONCENTRATING	☑ SUCCESSFUL & DELIVERS
☑ EXCESSIVE WORRYING	☑ ALWAYS OFFERS TO HELP
☑ IRRITABILITY	☑ HIGHLY ORGANIZED
☑ TROUBLE SLEEPING	☑ TENDENCY TO OVERTHINK
☑ PANIC ATTACKS	☑ MIND RACING/ALWAYS ON
☑ SOCIALLY ANXIOUS	☑ NEEDS REASSURANCE
☑ SENSE OF DREAD	☑ HAS DIFFICULTY SAYING NO
☑ RESTLESSNESS	☑ PEOPLE PLEASER
☑ MUSCLE TENSION	☑ MENTALLY FATIGUED

Did it ever occur to you that the high functioning isn't as noticeable because of the society we live in and the goals we chase covet these characteristics? Just because they are adorned doesn't make them healthy. Being high-functioning on the outside while struggling deeply on the inside is the state of many. This is what that can look like to others versus what is happening inside.

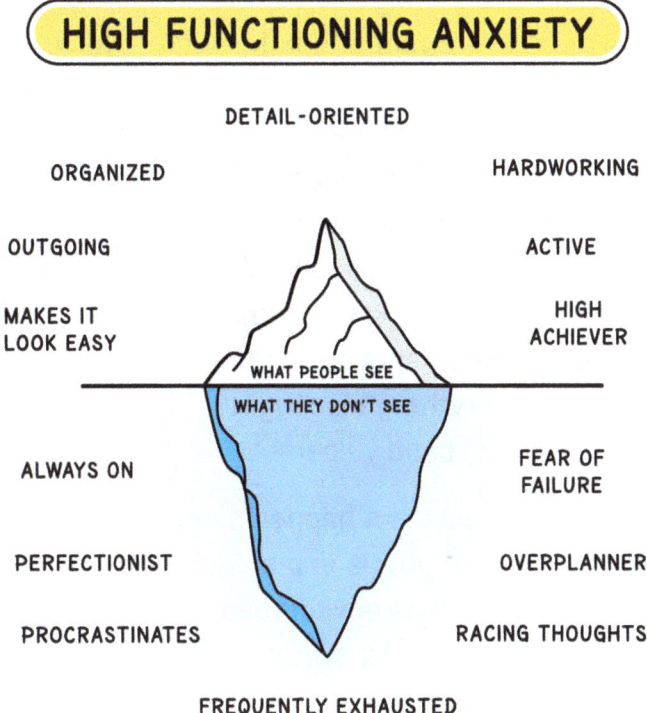

This is a deeply vulnerable moment for me, and I hope this iceberg is eye-opening for you. The entire time I thought all these outward attributes that were praised by others were really my strengths, they were tied to my inner weaknesses. I believed that because I got the validation on the outside, I was on the right path. I knew the truth of how I felt on the inside, that's why this whole work starts with you, and looking internally. I had to come to grips with the truth of what was happening. My ability to be organized was simply a result of overplanning. My seemingly busy schedule and active nature led me to procrastinate because I was overwhelmed mentally, so I self-destructed. Lastly, all the achievements I acquired acted as a mask for my perfectionism. What about you?

Slow down for a moment and ask yourself: have you been running fast on the treadmill of high-functioning anxiety and still haven't gotten any closer to your goals and dreams? Some of us even blame legitimate things like our job and schedule or the obligations to our families. But let's be real, we know it's not that because it's been years and you've made time for everything else, right? It's time to be honest and vulnerable.

> *"I'm an artist and I'm sensitive about my shit."*
> *-Erykah Badu*

Of course, this doesn't just happen overnight; there are contributing factors that put us in a unique position to operate this way. Factors such as environmental stress can also play a role, potentially triggering symptoms. Perfectionism is tied directly to a high-functioning anxiety disorder, which would only create more plans to feed that perfectionism. In some cases, it may be due to genetics or an individual's brain chemistry. One of the main factors for me was childhood trauma and, more specifically, the need to be perfect to gain parental approval while also becoming codependent, which turned into a people pleaser. It bred a high-achieving, reliable practitioner for others and an idealist of his own, who was a dependable leader to the world, yet achieved no lasting accomplishments in what mattered most to him. Whew, I'll unpack that when we get to perfectionism for more understanding.

Do you see how deep this can get for some of us? I am not providing a justification for why you haven't started, but I am linking a reason as to why we often foster plans and romanticize them, or busy ourselves with others' needs to the point where our own needs are never fulfilled.

Deep traumas can cause anxiety and fears about the unknown, and that fear can present itself in the form of overplanning and never actualizing. **Putting your potential into a plan that doesn't move isn't any better than never realizing your potential**. It ends the same…self-sabotage.

We are setting ourselves up for failure if we are aware of this issue and continue down the same path anyway. The tricky thing about self-sabotage is that, in this instance, it also requires cognitive dissonance because, while you are scared to fail, which is why you haven't started, you will simultaneously self-sabotage, which only ends in the same inevitable failure. How ironic!

Don't hinder your success with all this overplanning any longer; you need to get off making obstacles on the roadmap ahead of time and just jump on the road!

CHAPTER 05

Are You Full Yet?

"Is there ever a point where all our consumption becomes all-consuming and keeps us in a state of paralysis?"

Planning requires absorbing tons of information to formulate a strategic method of execution. How much more information do you need? You are full of ideas! Greatness oozes out of you as you continue to load yourself up on the substance that feeds your inner desires. Every time something new comes up, you add it to your vision board. Although you have your plan, you extend your mission and expand your vision whenever a new encounter leaves you inspired. When you see that life-changing quote or post online, you race to screenshot it, repost it, save it to favorites, and work it in some way with all your ideas. Day in and day out, you scroll on social media, soaking up the content and collective consciousness of others through their expressed thoughts online, and you love it! So much time is spent doom-scrolling, saving, swiping, and sharing that it feels like you need a break from your full-time job. You know how we do though, we justify it all by saying we are learning from

The Planning Procrastinating Perfectionist

others, getting to know our audience, and building our brand while staying in touch with the market.

We absorb so much information on a relatively quick basis that it becomes all-consuming and hard to process. Couple that with our desire to keep up with all the information in our respective fields. We go from watching YouTube videos, listening to multiple podcasts, running through threads of tweets and scores of Instagram videos, participating in like-minded Discord groups, deep-diving on TikTok, engaging in Live feeds, reading books, attending webinars and masterminds, and buying courses. Some of you have done a combination of these things, while others have completed them all, and yet you are still here. So, I just have one question. **Are you full yet?**

How much more motivation, inspiration, innovation, and acceleration do you need? You have become obese on the wealth of knowledge and content material you have. When will you finally make it a reality and release it for yourself? I want to be very clear that the actions mentioned above are part of your process of growing and evolving into the beast you were meant to be. They are part of the journey that triggers you to finally release what you have been 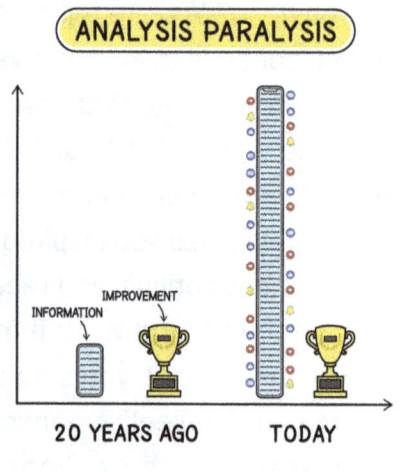 meant to contribute to the world. Although it is all part of the road, they are not the final resting place.

If you are reading this book, I know you have made a pit stop in your learning, and as a result, your growth is stunted. **You have made a bed out of a benchmark and a rest stop into your final resting place!** I empathize with you because I, too, have been in this cyclical place. Why do we eat past our full point? The simple answer is because we want to, and it tastes good.

Your Insatiable Appetite

Let's talk about it for a second. Did you know there are hunger hormones in the body called ghrelin that are released through the stomach, which send signals to your brain to tell you to keep eating? It creates an appetite in you even if you are already full. Interestingly enough, if you don't need to feed, you will only eat what is pleasurable! We have convinced ourselves that doing something is better than nothing, and so day and night, we consume what pleases us.

If you are stuck in this stage, you may have become obese on the obvious: learning from others, building your networks, investing in yourself, and remaining inspired and creative. Eventually, however, those practices become substitutionary mind-numbing pleasures that distract you more than executing your own plans. Do not fall into this trap it is bogus progress. You fear the risk of starting something for yourself and have become fat from your own appetite. Meanwhile, you are making everyone else rich by buying what they put the work into, selling to people like you. Don't be that person. Your lack of motion is monetizing their content platforms and paying their rent. Be smarter than that. Get what you need from what you acquire, and use it as motivation to start.

You'll never see me brag at the end of the year about how many books I've read because my approach is different. I take my time with them like I would with a good meal because I want to savor every part and observe how it leaves me feeling and what lessons I can take from it. I want to taste every flavor and texture instead of rushing through. When I finish a good book that boosts my knowledge in my field of expertise, it's often highlighted like a coloring book because of the number of notes I've made inside. Typically, I complete any homework or chapter-end assignments and incorporate them into my personal routines. Then, I apply and test new tactics in my business and life to see if they work best for me, and I share what I've learned with others.

Speaking of food, appetites, and digestion, can I be honest for a second? I hate small plates. That's a real thing.

It's one thing to overconsume content and never take action; however, we often serve ourselves small plates. Once you're finally motivated and educated, go big and go hard. One of my pet peeves is when someone is on the verge of pursuing something they're passionate about, and when they tell others, they downplay it and minimize their passion. You know how it goes: "Oh, I just own a little boutique, that's all," or "I don't really do much, I just started a small service that does ABC for XYZ." After all the planning, procrastination, and perfection, is this how you want to present yourself in a room? You've spent months and paychecks on education and personal growth just to show us your small plate? Take up space in the room because your idea is huge, and it deserves that. Face it, you might be doing too much.

I've been here and I've seen it.

There was a time when I literally wore four to five different hats in my younger years and managed it well. My ability to manage each thing separately and consistently in its respective place was something to admire. Some tasks required me to build teams, others needed automation and subcontractors, while some required my creative input rather than my physical presence. I was showing up and giving attention and intention to each respective area until the people closest to me uttered those deadly words, "I think you have too much on your plate."

I sat in silence and thought about it, and started to believe them, so I began to chop down what I was doing because I didn't want to miss the plot of it all. I even questioned if it was too much for them or me. One day, it dawned on me that I don't have too much on my plate; I just have a bigger appetite for success, and my approach to execution looks different, which was difficult for outsiders to digest. With a more diverse palette than others due to my inherent nature, the process looked different, and that's okay, as long as everything aligns in its perfect time with structure. This is where I derived the notion and phrase "I hate small plates."

You see, we cannot be naïve to believe that all of us can do everything at once *and* do it well. That is a recipe for disaster and a fast track to burnout. However, you are an untapped well that is still waters with the ability to quench the thirst of your respective audience. I don't believe in multi-tasking because the definition is to focus on multiple things at once, which the human mind cannot do efficiently. I believe you can focus on different aspects of a project for specific periods to achieve a positive outcome. If I use my 24 hours and split them up into six different time slots for high energy and focus on different tasks, I win the day. On the outside, it looks as if I'm all over the place and spreading myself thin, when in actuality, I am hyper-focused and seizing the day. Carpé Diem, as they say. But was it all beneficial?

This took me a long time to learn, and I'm hoping to alleviate you from the pain of that lesson. I've seen much of this exemplified in women and their ability to show up fully in multiple roles at the same time. Particularly after childbirth, I have watched beautiful strong women who are famished and exhausted, still find the strength to get up and feed their newborn. Amidst tending to her spouse, still responding to the demands of other children, answering calls from her parents, navigating household duties, and preparing to go back to work. Women, in particular, demonstrate this ability to me day in and day out. You can excel in more than one area, but each requires its own timing and attention.

A Jack of All Trades is a Master of None...

Whenever I heard this phrase, it took me from soaring with the stars and planted my feet back on the ground. "Come on, Dante you have to be a master of one thing." There are eight billion people on the planet, do you know how difficult it is to be good at so many different things and find success? There have been many times where I start to conform back to the preconditioned mindset that I was not made for more. However, upon further research, I discovered that the idiom above, which others had used to limit me, was incomplete; like much of history, it had been altered. The full sentence reads as such:

> **"A jack of all trades is a master of none,
> but oftentimes better than a master of one."**

Wait a minute, so the statement used to box up my talents and niche me down is actually an abridged reductionist viewpoint and extrapolated from a larger phrase intended as a compliment, not an insult? Sorry, I geeked out for a minute, but my mind was blown!

This full phrase simply means, if an ordinary person has multiple specialties, they may not be the best or the top at any one because they are a generalist. However, because he/she is so uniquely skilled and gifted in multiple areas, their collective benefit will often outweigh a person who is great at just one thing. This was never intended to be negative but to celebrate your diversity and limitless ability!

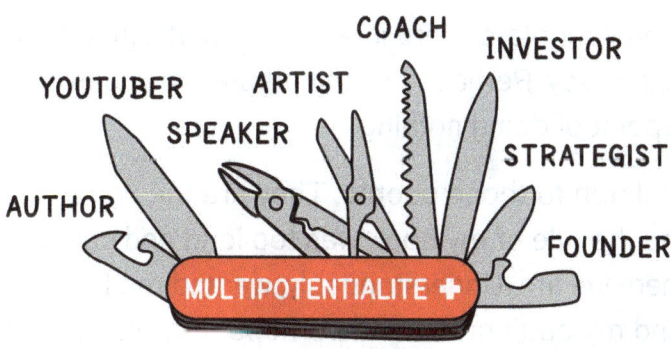

Through research, I have discovered this is more than just a Renaissance person, a polymath, or a multi-talented individual.

They called us a "Jack of All Trades," but the term used today in certain circles is a Multipotentialite. This correctly defines a person's inherent nature to pursue many passions through all their skills. Within that, if they execute on them and derive titles, they are identified as a multihyphenate, which is why you will see things like (Author – Founder – Coach). They all exist within that person, and it was all brought forth due to them executing new, clear, informed, and insightful information extracted from the chaos, revealing their hidden potential.

After all that time of my convincing myself that I couldn't walk and chew gum. The generation that came before me was accustomed to attending college and holding one job for decades until retirement. When they witnessed you at your full-time job, hosting online content, while saving money for the property to launch your business, they couldn't fathom it. They said you were doing too much and that meant you were destined for failure. You can't possibly be a co-founder of a company and a blogger while singing on the weekends. How are you an author, a chairman, a full-time YouTuber, and a speaker? You have too much on your plate. Here is a smaller plate, just do that one thing…they say. Perhaps this contributed to you overplanning to the point of doing nothing.

I don't listen to those people. They are the same ones that told me the title of my book was too long and confusing and well, here we are. Understandably, wanted me to niche down and find my audience – and perhaps they weren't wrong in their thinking, but I speak to multiple audiences. So, I needed to find others like me who understood what it was like to be a Multipotentialite and speak to our lived and shared experiences.

In finding that community, I'd like to introduce you to an amazing and creative mentor who has been instrumental in this journey. Matt Gottesman is the founder of "The Niche Is You," and he also hosts a daily podcast with the same name that can be found everywhere. I recommend following him and listening to his bite-sized daily episodes, filled with gems that help you feel seen and know you are aligned. We are all experts at living our own lives, and we can never fail at our own purpose. We may need some redirection or gentle guidance, but always stay in your lane and drive that extra mile as you surpass the traffic of groupthink.

I'm here to tell you that out of the abundance of your one idea may flow multiple waves and different lanes that will create a newer version of you. You may begin to acquire assets that generate income in a more passive manner. Perhaps you become an Airbnb host by owning a property. Or you could start renting out leased vehicles through a ride-sharing app like Turo. You may even get into owning vending machines. With ownership of all these assets, you can apply a system and strategy to them to make them passive income generators. You would still be a person who has a podcast for entrepreneurs; however, you also generate passive income through vending, car rentals, and Airbnb rentals. That makes you a beast with a big ass plate, and each item is being tended to well. You are investing in assets and digesting success, all while increasing your knowledge and value in a capitalistic society that has relegated you to a small niche. Do not be scared to launch into those uncharted waters, just be smart.

When I say, "be smart," before executing and scaling up with systems and automation, you have to first align all of these things. How do we take everything that's on your plate that you want to accomplish, along with the tasks associated with them, and get them done? We need to introduce a strategy. After all, you are only one person, and not being organized is the fastest way to fail. I have been utilizing this simple matrix for over 15 years, and it has helped me when I've had more ideas and aspirations than time and money.

Consider the Eisenhower Matrix:

This matrix helps us make decisions about items, tasks, and desires that are both important and urgent by grouping them and determining the best course of action. To become a powerhouse with all that you've consumed, apply hyperfocus mixed with intentional organization. This isn't overplanning, but rather understanding your capacity and limitations and devising a strategy to address what is not only important but also urgent first, and then moving forward from there. Keep an eye out for this when we discuss timing later in a future chapter. Take note that it's okay to have a plan to do more than one thing, so as long as everything isn't crammed into the top left quadrant. We will revisit this concept in a later chapter.

In traditional business, for quantifying metrics, we may need to niche down so we can conquer that arena before scaling. My advice to you is to do the one thing well and build systems and processes so it can be maintained as you evolve into the next phase of who you are going to be. I love that for you as a Multipotentialite, if that's who you are. That fierce person who meets challenges head-on, executes, and keeps eating because they have an appetite only for envisioned success, not short-term pleasures. The Theory of Moore I hold shows me not to be satisfied with being just a one-trick pony, but also don't be the clown – own the fucking circus and franchise it while you're at it!

We are full, not just with potential or knowledge, but with greatness that has been planned, perfected, and put off for long enough. We are full off of the passion and drive within us, with the direction from others. We are full and ready to show up in a big way for ourselves, so we can stop counting the pennies and the plates of others. Are you full yet? Execute, and keep eating to build your appetite for success. You can't afford to wait any longer.

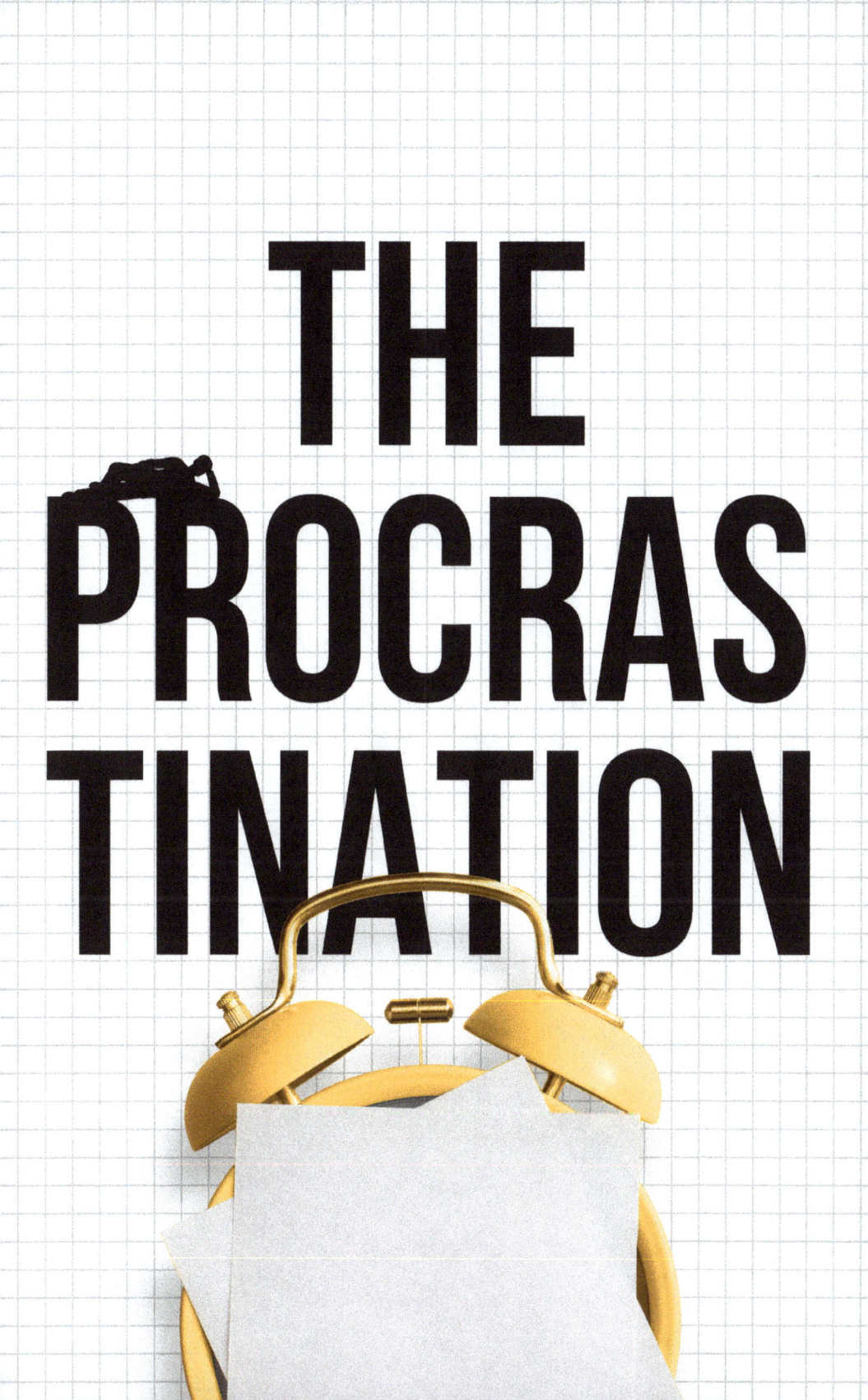

CHAPTER 06

The Procrastination

"If you're afraid to fail, that means you are afraid to start."

—Kevin Hart

In Chapter 1, we spent a great deal of time discussing feelings and emotions along with why they are important. Ignoring the reasons of how we respond to emotion or interpret them in our feelings makes us numb to the behaviors that follow them and thus incapable of correcting them. We will take a healthy look at procrastination in this chapter and examine how our thoughts inform our feelings, which in turn influence our actions and behavior. Viewing the process from this state is what would be defined as using a cognitive behavioral lens. You cannot identify or begin to defeat your procrastination if you don't start with a healthy examination of yourself: Start With You. Remember, the hard work is the heart work and that always comes first.

What is Procrastination?

Procrastination is defined as the unnecessary act of delaying or postponing something that must be done, whether by decision or in action. In many cases this is because the action that is required may be either unpleasant or boring.

Each person does not procrastinate for the same reasons, nor do they function in the same ways while delaying their tasks. Applying a one size fits all approach to procrastination does a disservice to critically investigating the source behind it for each individual and how it presents itself. The motivations and modalities to which procrastination is expressed when studied unveils itself in a myriad of ways.

Leaning on the model from the book, *It's About Time – The Six Styles of Procrastination* by Linda Sapadin and Jack Maguire, I'd like us to dive deeper into exploring these forms for true understanding.

According to Sapadin, there are six different types of procrastinators divided into two separate groups based off their drivers:

- The Worrier
- The Perfectionist
- The Over-Doer
- The Crisis-Maker
- The Dreamer
- The Defier

Group 1: Anxiety Based

1. **The Worrier** – *"If I try, then I'll fail."*

    Fears a task being too difficult for them to succeed before they even attempt it. They are overly cautious and afraid and would rather never start and stay comfortable rather than start and face the possibility of failure.

2. **The Perfectionist** – *"If it's not perfect, I'm a failure."*

    Will often delay starting any tasks that have less-than-perfect or ideal circumstances, coupled with a precise plan. If it can't be done perfectly, it won't be done at all.

3. **The Over-Doer** – *"If I don't accomplish all of this, then I'm a failure."*

    Overcommits to a lot of projects for others while pushing back what they need to do for themselves. As a result, they don't prioritize their needs and tie their worth to accomplishing the impossible task of doing everything, resulting in fatigue, burnout, then ultimately failure.

Group 2: Boredom/Low Frustration Tolerance Based

4. **The Dreamer** – *"I shouldn't have to work this hard to fulfill my dreams."*

   Loves to live in the abstract high-level creative nature of ideas but when it comes to dealing with the details they'd rather opt out. They believe things should just happen for them naturally and they struggle or avoid taking high focused actions to bring their dreams to fruition. They prefer to rely more on their gifts and ignore the grind.

5. **The crisis-maker** – *"I shouldn't have to do this right now; I work better under pressure."*

   Believes pressure is when they produce their best results. They need the stress of the deadline to give them motivation to finally start what they have been delaying out of boredom. They overestimate their ability and don't acknowledge all the factors they can't account for which usually results in their work being rushed as time expires.

6. **The Defier** – *"I shouldn't have to do this task at all."*

   A rebel who resists change, the rules, and what they are supposed to do so they can feel in control of their own schedule and timeline. They delay the necessary because they feel that they can, and out of frustration, they despise having to even deal with the task at all. The work to them may seem mundane, so their mindset is fixed on insubordination.

These six types have distinct motivations and root causes. The first three types are anxiety-based, while the last three are based on boredom or what is referred to as low frustration tolerance. Anxiety procrastinators experience heightened stress imagining the varying results of their work and labor. Boredom or low frustration tolerance, procrastinators encounter stress through imagining the experience of the work ahead of them. The first is overwhelmed with anticipation of the results, while the second is underwhelmed by the experience, but stress is unavoidable for all types of procrastinators.

Anxiety-based procrastinators have a deep fear of failure at their core. That overwhelming prospect of failing and not meeting the expectations of others and themselves forces them into a state of overanalyzing. This cycle turns into a delay of the necessary action with avoidance elected as a coping mechanism for comfort and a blanket of security. What starts off as temporary relief from this crippling anxiety manifests itself as long-lasting procrastination. The anxiety-based procrastinator is constantly running from the fear of the anticipated results and trying their best to not make a decision that will lead to their failure.

Boredom/Low Frustration Tolerance procrastinators exhibit a different emotion, anger, which is more closely tied to the process of completing their goal. It comes off as boredom or frustration, but it is embedded in the belief that they are somehow above the process or the task itself. If the tasks are repetitive and mundane, they struggle to complete them, often putting them off for as long as possible. They could be incredibly talented or remarkably intelligent, and this may add to the frustration of taking the next step.

It is likely that a person can identify with more than one type of procrastination style. Where do you see yourself among the six types? Ask yourself: Why don't I stick to my routines, or have my presentation ready the night before, or start the task when I said I would? Is it anxiety, boredom, or frustration? Maybe it's a combination of both.

Within me, I've seen the Worrier emerge when it came to things like ending relationships that no longer served me or my growth. The Perfectionist grandstands when it comes to the entire idea of *The Theory of Moore* and my transition to the West Coast. I've seen the Over-Doer enter the room, taking on all my family's problems to be good enough for them, but not enough for myself.

The Dreamer also steps in whenever I share my vision board and five-phase plan with others, and they are captivated. I've seen the Crisis-Maker emerge with the creation of this very book, as friends kept asking about my next move. So, when I locked myself in a hotel room to finish the first manuscript in four days, I felt a sense of achievement because the pressure of a last-minute deadline served as a mental boost and could make a great story someday. Lastly, the Defier appears in me every time I face tough financial times and have to work for others or corporate America again to support my dreams.

Reclaiming Your Time

Usually, I've found that the best day for a procrastinator to perform is "Someday." The ideal time for their activation is never now, it's always later – someday. The day that is always in the future and yet never arrives is tomorrow and they love it there. Don't forget your discipline in these moments and how crucial it is. Discipline only operates in today; it doesn't understand any other language. It doesn't grieve over yesterday or overestimate tomorrow. It exists just enough for today to activate you in this very moment.

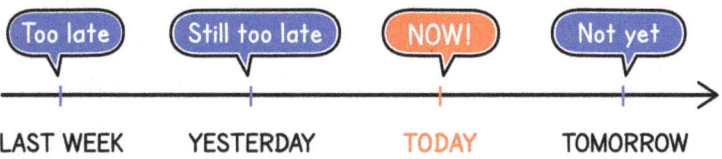

Operating on the "Someday" calendar and abandoning daily disciplines continually could have a person wasting the majority of their day and towards the end of it, they feel sorry for themselves for how they spent their 24 hours. Then they make another plan for the next time and do it all over again. This state of existing is concerning because there will come a time where we all run out of days and moments.

There was a popular home décor item circulating on social media a while back of a unique piece of wall art that was intended to be motivational for procrastinators like you and I. It was called "My Life In Weeks." The entire piece was filled with empty dots and each dot represented a week in a given year and the years were sectioned down into decades to fill the canvas. Essentially, one's whole life could be seen at a glance, represented by empty dots. For every week that passes the instructions were for you to fill in a dot. Your life in weeks. I know for me, I couldn't bear to walk past this every morning, actively filling out a dot week after week watching my time pass me by all while knowing I am stuck in my head and struggling to remove my destructive thought patterns.

Life is for living and not for limits! We have destructive thought patterns that limit our forward motion and when deeply engrained they create our limiting beliefs. **A limiting belief is a false belief or set of false beliefs that we hold that constrain us from achieving our desires.** These beliefs can come in many forms, but they are erected to protect us from the pain and fears on the other side of them. With respect, they confine us from any forward mobility or living out our dreams, desires, and destiny. In this way can one see how the statement *"I've got time"* is a limiting belief and a popular one at that! Our limiting beliefs create the construct for the perfect snow globe where our glass ceiling never shatters, but our excitement only rises upward to condense into disappointment from the clouds of our despair and false inadequacy, raining right back onto our heads. I say, it's time to uproot those limiting beliefs and bring back the sunshine!

This is your life and you are in control of what you believe and how you manage your days. As the poet William Ernest Henley once said *"I am the master of my fate. I am the captain of my soul.*" So, steer that soul towards greatness without limitations and we start that by dismantling old belief patterns. Your life is more than a series of dots or blips on a radar. When you take back control as opposed to remaining on autopilot, in a short period of time you can fulfill some of your wildest imaginations. You are still human and some of those imaginations may include a desired getaway with family or an occasional outing. A full life and a long life are not always synonymous – so I challenge you today to try to live fully past your limitations with respect to who and where you are!

IT'S NOT ABOUT THE YEARS IN YOUR LIFE...

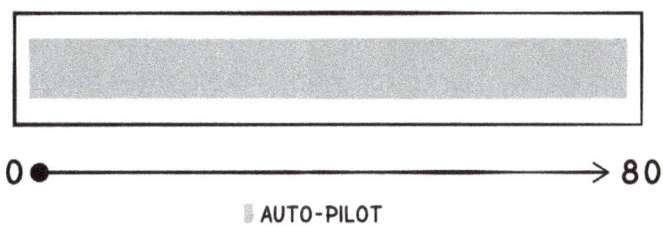

...IT'S ABOUT THE LIFE IN YOUR YEARS

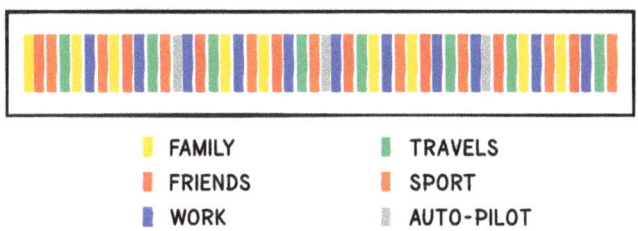

However, you choose to spend your day, do it with intention. Your goals may not always take priority, and that's ok. Reclaim the time that is yours. We require balance in order to experience the vast joys life has to offer. Others from the outside may misinterpret your delays to the things that matter more to them as slothfulness but don't let that noise distract you or trick you into falling for another belief that is not your own.

YOUR PROCRASTINATION IS NOT A RESULT OF YOU SIMPLY BEING LAZY!

I need you to hear me and hear me clearly. You are not lazy! You may be paralyzed by fear or pushing off the inevitable out of frustration or busyness, but you are not lazy. Reading this book this far shows you have what it takes and are committed to progressing forward, but you must meet it with action while there is still time!

In the words of the rapper Emmanuel Lambert, "Once your moment is passed, your moment's the past – then poof! You can't revive it or hold it…" We are engaging in all these mental gymnastics in our heads and wasting time, and for whom are we doing it? Who are we waiting for? Who are we explaining to? This all starts with you, and you must understand no one else is responsible for what you do next. No one.

CHAPTER 07

No One...

This is the stage of your journey that will bring you the most freedom to help you live outrageously, knowing you're made for more and that your time is now.

Do you know who is on the other side waiting for your delayed perfect plan to fail?

> No one.
> No one is waiting.
> No one.

Your entire system of beliefs, projected false realities, and anxiety-induced self-deprecating talk, you've immersed yourself in has stalled you from starting. You need a gentle wake-up call and reminder that the world is not waiting for you or paying you any mind. Who are you trying to impress?

> No one.
> No one is waiting.
> No one is watching.
> No one is critically analyzing.

No one is over judging.
No one.

No one cares.
No one is interested.
No one thinks twice about it.
No one knows it even it exists.
No one knows you.
No one has a reason to believe.
No one sees your behind the scenes.
No one.

No one is responsible.
No one is liable.
No one is expected to understand.
No one is at fault for delays.
No one is to blame for redirection.
No one holds the guilt for time lost.
No one can give birth to what is inside of you.
No one has the passion you have.
No one can live your life for you.
No one.

When it's time to get started, you need to embrace the hard truths that:

No one is ever ready.
No one starts out great.
No one fully conquers fear.
No one has planned for every threat.

No one releases it perfect.
No one knows the best time to go.
No one ever has it all figured out.
No one does it without failing up.
No one knows the all the outcomes.
No one is an expert the first time.
No one can do what you do.
No one can control the future.
No one can limit the impact.
No one can take it from you.
No one.

To conclude this point, allow me to show you a shocking visual illustration of what the world looks like when you try anything and make a mistake.

THE WORLD BEFORE AND AFTER

YOU'VE MADE A MISTAKE

What a sobering, challenging, and yet gut-wrenching wake-up call. We often project our fears and doom onto no one. The world will go on despite our mistakes or failures. We have drawn our own future as a freehand face that looks like failure. This is what we conjured up to keep us from pursuing what is within us. We have drawn up a person, a time, a place in life, of non-existence to become our arch nemesis. They feed us all the answers to our questions and doubts. Telling us to stay in our collective cocoons just a little while longer while the world keeps spinning. We are alive, yet not truly living. It's time to be brought back to life.

I see I may need to bring out the high voltage charges needed to resuscitate and pump this heart with some heavy shockwaves of truth. Brace yourself, I'm Dr. Moore, and I've been through this and in your same position, and it hurts, but you will live again. Procrastination gave you a brief flatline, but don't worry here comes the first shockwave of truth.

Shockwaves

---CLEAR---

1. **Your humility is ego**

    Self-inflated importance has you stuck in a rotation. You delay your big idea, don't share it with others, over-value your learning and planning, while simultaneously putting the end goal on the back burner. Whenever you're asked about it you minimize it as if it's not the aim that keeps you up for days. This humility you're projecting about not executing is, in reality, a false pride disguised as a beggar yet riddled with thoughts of supreme self-importance.

Do you really think the entire world is waiting for you to unleash your gifts? No one is waiting. They will only respond to the level at which we project it into the environment. Are you arrogant enough to believe that you can make this thing you hold perfect? You honestly believe you will be the first person to create something with no issues, mishaps, or failures, huh? Sure, they say it takes a little bit of delusion to make something great happen, but I think we are a little deep off the reservation here. Keep setting small goals because of your big ego, and you will miss out on everything that awaits you.

---CLEAR---

2. **You are a coward**

    This is not negative reinforcement; this is freedom juice, so drink it all up. By definition, you are a coward. Not because you lack the basic foundational courage and bravery to stand boldly even against your fears and perceived threats. No, you are first ego-driven to think you will have an idea that could be released and be perfect. That ego, however, is cloaked in humility, so no one can hold you accountable for a failure of execution. You are a coward for a more fundamental reason.

    This world and marketplace need whatever it is you are bringing to the table. Don't withhold it! Cowards stay inside, always perfecting something in an imperfect world. For whom? The invisible crowd? The silent parental voice? Cowards like us keep waiting for 'someday' and 'one day' as the launch date, instead of today. This cowardice lacks bravery in the face of great strain and struggle. We are cowardly enough to stay hidden and free from the feeling of rejection and worst of all—failure.

---CLEAR---

3. **All of us fail**

Anyone who has ever done anything, whether remembered or not, has failed. Every great success is littered with failure, for they are the building steps of the stairway to success. The most prudent lessons for those now thriving came off the heels of failure and defeat. The moment any of us manifests in public what we have harvested in our hearts, we open it up to the possibility of failure. That is the point, for what is life without the looming thought and presence of death? All of us who have contributed anything to the world have faced and dealt with failure, but that does not mean it has to be final.

You will fail repeatedly, and that should be welcomed and expected. There are lessons hidden in failure that thousands of books and courses on development could never teach you. That's why listening to a rising entrepreneur streaming live about their failures and how they pivoted offers more insight—learning from their experience. The lessons we gain from others' failures are valuable, but those we learn from our own failures are priceless! You will fail, my friend, but that's how you succeed.

In plain visuals, all the shit you've been through that have culminated your failures, is the only reason you have the ability to build blocks of success now! The glue holding it all together is the failure that you despised.

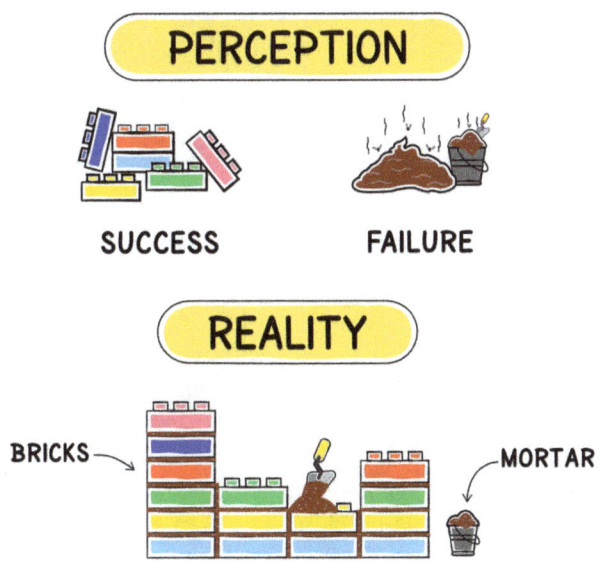

I hope you can hear the wisdom in these words. Your heart may often align with the delusions of your mind, but these are the shockwaves you needed. Come alive! I hope that by now, these words have jolted some life into your body, giving you the energy needed to defeat the next part of your struggle, which is your mind. Let's keep this momentum and hijack the mind back to take hold of some tangible ways to rework our thinking!

CHAPTER 08

What Are You Thinking?

"Don't think. Just do."
—Unknown

So, we've talked about you, your habits, your overplanning, your procrastinating, and the shockwaves your mind needs to get unstuck and take action. This chapter will help you understand how your mind works. There is a complicated highway in your brain that contains billions of nerve cells and neurotransmitters producing electric signals that fire off one another to form thoughts. Just to think is deeply complex in itself.

We are always thinking, but is that all we are doing?

When you share your passions, do you frame it in a certain way? Have you ever said the words "I was thinking about..." before sharing your idea? I'm sure you have. Then you serve it up on a small plate, based on your fear so as to ensure no one has any real clue on how to hold you to definitive labor or deadlines for execution. I guess you're still operating on that "someday" calendar, huh? Now I'm no neuroscientist or cartographer, but I can imagine that this is what the complex brain of any overthinking procrastinator looks like as a sequence:

The planning folds very seamlessly into procrastination. Plan jumps to plan to more plans, and the cycle continues.

We have highlighted the different ways why it happens, the different types of procrastinators, and what it looks like. Now I'd like to unravel how it happens in relation to time. If we follow this pattern long enough, you will look up and years will have gone by, wondering how you allowed yourself to be on autopilot, watching your life pass you by.

Historian and author by the name of Cyril Northcote Parkinson, who described a phenomenon experienced amongst many people with consideration to personal productivity called Parkinson's Law. It states that the complexity of a task tends to grow the more time is allotted for its completion. Not only its complexity but the work itself expands so as to fill the available time for its completion.

This expansion in essence means that if you give yourself a week to do a task that takes an hour to complete, then that single one-hour task will grow in complexity and difficulty to fill the time.

Thus, the easy bridge to procrastination is born. Parkinson's Law can work both ways, where if you place yourself on the 'someday' calendar, you are preparing to procrastinate. Let's look at the Eisenhower 'Time Management' Matrix again to determine which group each task ought to be placed in to ensure you plan *and* maximize your time accordingly.

If you claim that your goals are important to you, then they should sit above the horizontal line and be categorized as either urgent or non-urgent. According to the matrix, if Parkinson's Law has caused you to allow more time for tasks to be completed, even if they are important to you, they are not a priority, which is why you scheduled them with more plans. This is not good for a procrastinator because, if left to our own devices, a day turns into a week, which turns into a year, and now we have filled all that time justifiably in our minds to complete in a year what should have been done in a day. Giving yourself too much time to do a simple task in a longer plan only makes it more complex, time-consuming, and ultimately, daunting and stressful. This creates anxiety or frustration.

This law works in the opposite way as well. If you give yourself too little time for a task that requires more time to execute you are now back to invoking what we discussed before in our planning chapter regarding the planning fallacy. This can produce a stress that makes you feel like you have to get it done, which frustrates you and then comes the defier or the crisis-maker trying to save you from the very problem you created. This is a vicious cycle.

Now What?

So, what is the fix? You have the Eisenhower Matrix and you understand Parkinson's Law, but that won't translate into action. Making a to-do list and telling yourself you are going to properly prioritize has been done before. Multiple journals, scheduling apps, notes on your phones, to-do lists, memos and reminders all over the place. We need tangibles to make this work for us no matter how big or small the task.

Here are some key principles to help you maximize the matrix:

1. **Use the Pareto Principle**

Focus on 20% of the tasks with all your effort that you know will produce 80% of the results that you desire. This can also be called the 80/20 effect, and it is the best way to prioritize using the matrix.

2. **Eat The Frog technique**

   This methodology suggests that you should do your most challenging task first in the morning, when your energy and willpower are at their highest. Knock it out first, and once you've tackled the worst thing first, it will multiply your efforts throughout the day.

3. **The Two-minute rule**

   To be efficient and interrupt a mountain of overwhelming items, this rule states that if a thing can be done in two minutes or less do it immediately. Eliminating all those smaller tasks quickly also releases a sense of accomplishment with each.

4. **1-3-5 rule**

   This is a proven productivity strategy, whether you are completing tasks or preparing your day. Identify 1 big goal to accomplish, 3 medium ones, and 5 small tasks. You can place them

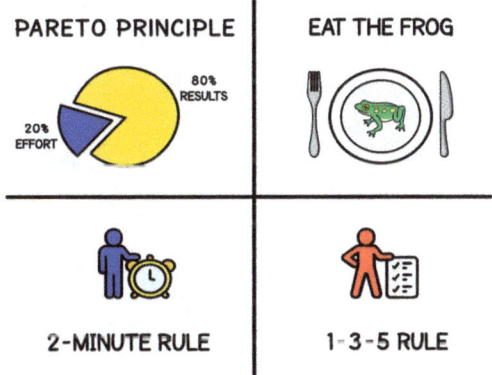

in their respective boxes and couple some of the other techniques above. Then, watch your day elevate!

Implement these into each of your days and your to-do lists and watch how rapid productivity starts to chase you. Time is your most valuable asset, and how you spend your time matters! Your 24 hours is no different than anyone else's but it is how we spend it that counts. Where do we place our intentions with the hours that are ours? As opposed to looking at how much other people gained and how far they've gotten, focus in on what you do with your 168 hours each week.

 My friends, the tools are right in front of us, now it's all about application. This is the tricky part because we've been down this road before, right? We started and stopped right before things too off. Now, we must finally approach the perfectionist within us all.

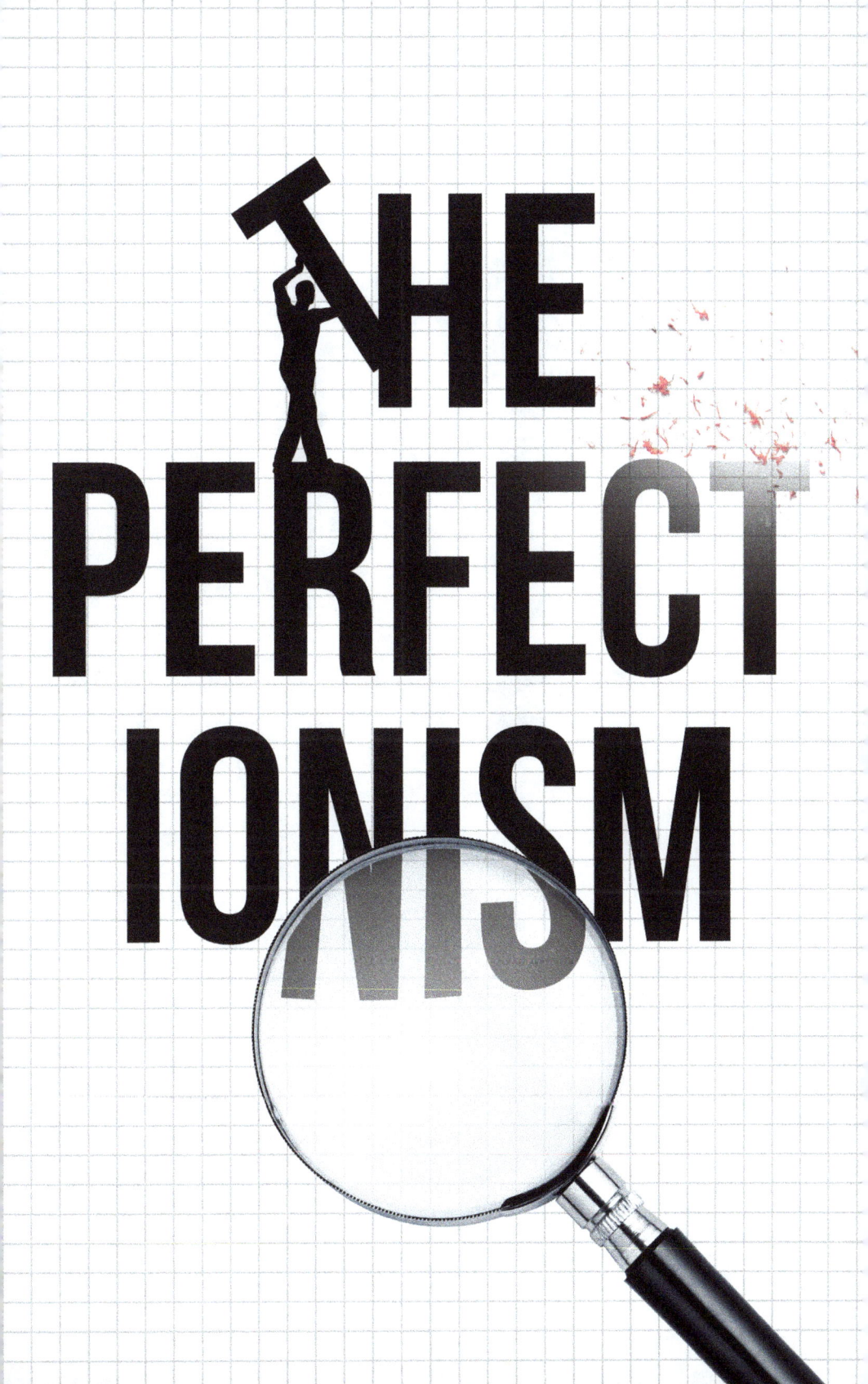

CHAPTER 09
The Perfectionism

"Perfection is an impossible destination."
–Tim Ferris

Allow me to begin with a confession. This has been the most challenging part of writing this book for me, as it is vast and expansive to cover. I have spent months compiling data, evaluating angles, and determining what is worth delivering that is substantive for you as the audience. Yet again, I find that my perfectionism is at play, so I have placed this section near the bottom, while labeling it the most important. It is a sickness for me as I told you and this condition of thinking something will turn out perfect from an imperfect being has crippled me. The following illustration looks a lot like my brain while I was writing this chapter:

Why did I do this? Why do we do this? It's such a strange phenomenon. Before we address the why, let's define the what, so we are all on the same page.

What is Perfectionism?

According to the American Psychological Association, it is the tendency to demand an extremely high or even flawless level of performance from others or oneself, in excess of what is required by the situation.

This is vital to understanding how many of us have inherited this perfectionist identity, because this topic is deeply layered and has roots that extend to many interconnected behaviors and modalities. Let's first see if we can spot some quick identifiers below. Check off whichever applies to you.

Here are 10 signs that you are a perfectionist:

1. You are highly critical of yourself and others.
2. You are sensitive to or find it hard to accept criticism and try to avoid it and you may get defensive with honest feedback.
3. You set unrealistic and unreasonable goals for yourself.
4. You have an "all or nothing" attitude but mask it by calling it "getting things done right" or "done in excellence or not at all."
5. You have a strong fear of failure.
6. Your main focus is results, and it bothers you when you don't meet them.
7. You have a hard time leaving responsibility to others in the form of delegating.
8. You experience bouts of depression when you haven't achieved the level you desired, and you have an internal FOMO (Fear of Missing Out) on what is for you.
9. You procrastinate to keep adding and don't start until you think things will be perfect.
10. You dwell and ruminate on mistakes and overthink scenarios that haven't occurred.

Are you feeling seen yet? How many of the signs sound like you? I bet you probably didn't even want to check off all the boxes that applied to you, because in your mind, what if someone found this book and saw that right? How would that make you look?

Some of us do this in our intimate journals where we are supposed to be most vulnerable. We will codify certain words or refine the less-than-perfect parts as if our private diaries would one day be on public display. The same happens with our to-do lists. We use that perfect pen and write them in with expert precision as if we are drafting a proposed bill to be presented to the floor of Congress. (*Refer now to the "No One" chapter.*)

This means you are obsessed with perfection! In all honesty, this stems from a fear of failure and judgment, and with that fear and judgment comes shame. This is where the perfectionist was born out of judgment and shame, and in most cases, we learned this at a very early age.

There is not one root cause of perfectionism that is exhibited in all our behavior patterns. Each individual may have several at work, but they stem from different sources. Examine below some of the most common causes of perfectionism:

> **1. Developmental factors** that cause perfectionism to occur:
>
> » Parenting styles that demand perfection or those who are supremely authoritarian or hypercritical. Neglect, dysfunction, or trauma in the household can also lead to developing a performative perfection model to gain the approval of parents/guardians.

When love is rooted in achievement and approval is only found in accomplishment, this breeds a survivalist perfectionist within a child.

» Educational pressure and the requirement to excel in class can create internal stressors that prompt constant performance. When high achievement is set early on within the developmental years as the standard, it places intense pressure to outperform their peers, while they are never satisfied with the results. In many cases, they cannot stop working towards a goal they will never achieve and may self-isolate within their own mind.

This one is extremely near to me when I look back, and do the heart work from within, I can see where the perfectionist in me was spawned. I was called the "chosen one" from an early age by my father, who had high standards, operated as an authoritative parent, and placed value on my accomplishments. Growing up in a black household, going to school, and hearing statements like "when you go into this school, you are a representation of me..." stuck with me throughout my childhood years. No one wants to disappoint or misrepresent their parents or an entire household by way of their conduct or performance. That pressure of not being a disappointment created not only a perfectionist but a people pleaser who was codependent on the validation to feel like I was enough. For 20 years, I was unable to place the words to this destructive mindset, but after much therapy and soul work, here we are. Take some time to reflect on your upbringing and the critical years of your development to see where the seeds of perfection were sown within you.

2. Cultural Factors that cause perfectionism to occur:

» The environment of the workplace where only high achievers and off-the-charts stats are celebrated. A consistent culture that says you are only as good as your last win, and you can be replaced if you don't perform can become a trigger. We believe our worth and value are tied to our accomplishments, capacity, and deliverables. In this case, we become tied to work highlights, seeing our names mentioned in emails and shout-outs, being complimented for our attire and attributes. Many of us become an entirely different person to keep up with the pace of perfection, and when we clock out, we are exhausted from the performance we've tried to maintain.

» Social pressures as a whole can create the perfectionist within. We often abandon what is natural to stay in line with current trends. This grind culture and watching social media influencers and celebrities rise to fame place the pressure on all of us to create the perfect content from our normal lives. The once-popular phrase "keeping up with the Joneses" is taken to a new level as we constantly compare ourselves to the entire world online. We essentially exchange our lives for a bad episode of Black Mirror, competing for likes, attention, and validation.

There are other factors that cannot be overlooked, which are simply inherent to who we are. While some are personality traits such as being driven, detail-oriented, or having a Type-A personality, there can also be other underlying factors. Those who have been diagnosed with anxiety disorders, obsessive-compulsive disorder (OCD), or ADHD may have a direct link to inducing perfectionism based on their brain chemistry.

We must acknowledge that all these factors can contribute to our perfectionism; however, regardless of how we arrived here, the goal is to break free from our own self-imposed limitations. In all these circumstances, our mind is feeding us information that we are not enough unless… (fill in the blank). As a result of that lie, we then perform perfectionism to become enough, and we enter a vicious cycle.

It's imperative to highlight this cycle because you need to see that it will never end. The simplified version was displayed initially, but what is really at work is much more nefarious. The flow cycle below illustrates that perfection is *not* the goal; it is, in fact, the obstacle. We are creating for ourselves the entryway to our own failure every time we gleefully hop on this merry-go-round.

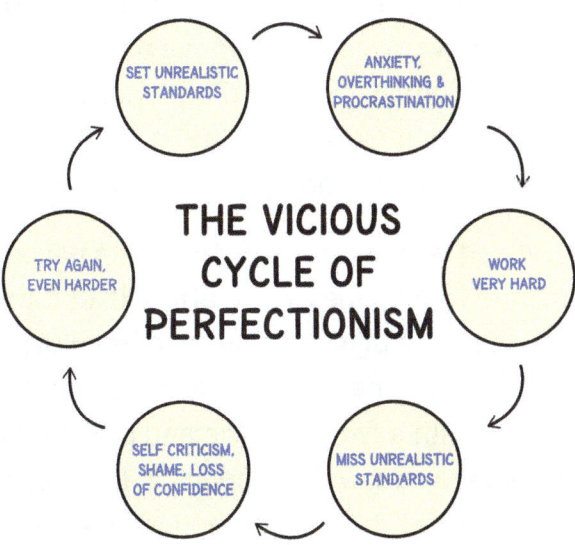

Take a moment to reflect on how draining this process is and consider where you find yourself at this very moment. Truthfully, there is no starting or ending point, as this is a recurring life cycle. You might think that this starts with setting unrealistic standards, but that may not be your start. You may be working very hard to meet those standards and plateauing, to where you realize you are unable to achieve that. The constant thirst to continually improve on what hasn't historically worked to achieve your goal is all-consuming.

Stuck in the Cycle

Quick story--I've worked many jobs in my life, and one of the many I enjoyed was my employment as a certified debt specialist at a FinTech company, where I assisted clients with getting out of massive amounts of unsecured debt, such as credit cards & loans. This illustration reminds me of what happened every day on my calls with these clients. I think about their stories of the debt cycle they were in, and I liken it to my own experiences and of those I know, so that I can have the empathy needed to aid them. We were all excited to get approved for our first few credit cards, right? We had all the plans to be financially responsible, but that's not how the game works.

What I've noticed is that many of my clients never really had a budget to determine if they could afford it, or if they had the discipline to keep their utilization below a harmful percentage. So, in those cases, you can never truly get out of it unless you pay it all off, but with a fixed income and constant expenses, that's highly unlikely. So, what happens in the meantime? The debt you owe grows with daily compounding interest, and you struggle to pay the minimums so that your credit doesn't decline further, while you try to afford basic necessities. It's safe to say you end up in survival mode.

What effect does that have on a person's mind? I've heard adults cry on the phone to me, and mothers tell me they can't afford childcare. I have heard widows discuss considering bankruptcy, and seniors tell me their Social Security isn't enough to help them. People from every demographic are living paycheck to paycheck because they had a perfect plan but didn't account for rising costs and procrastinated on repayment. Now, they are stuck in a never-ending cycle until they hit their limit.

Are you catching my drift here? Chasing perfection is just like a novice using credit cards. It will cost you more than you can afford to pay and take you further away from the goal than you ever anticipated.

You are stuck in the cycle—you can't get out. Clinicians, neuroscientists, and psychologists all talk about being stuck or getting unstuck when it comes to overcoming perfectionism. The term "The Stuck" is perfect because no matter how hard you try, you can't escape due to your own limiting beliefs and excuses. But who actually *wants* to stay stuck?

Britt Frank, the author of *"The Science of Stuck,"* proposes that there are hidden rewards to unhealthy habits, almost embedded within the drive that motivates that behavior. The thought really got me thinking about what I gain from the things I loathe, even if it is at the lowest vibrating parts of myself. She suggests some of the benefits could be feelings of familiarity, comfort, risk management, control, and even image preservation. Perhaps what guides our behavior when we jump into that cycle, much like with credit cards, is that our search for hidden rewards keeps us feeling secure.

In the book, Frank makes a profound statement: "Our brains are wired for survival, not happiness. Our nervous systems are trained to conserve as much energy as possible. Staying stuck is an efficient use of resources when the goal is survival. Staying stuck is problematic when the goal is productivity."

So, I ask you, what is your real goal? You can be protected in your perfect scenario and exist in survival mode, getting by on the minimums, or you can pay your dues and live free and thriving! **The decision is and has always been yours.**

The reason we get stuck in a loop is that, in some ways, we benefit from it, and we have inappropriately tied our worth to being perceived as perfect. Whether the pressures were internal, familial, or societal, the seeds have germinated and have taken deep root within us, and they drive every action. Outside of us, people applaud our effort and commitment to pursuing excellence, but you and I know the real truth, don't we? We never wanted to be on this wild ride of never producing and always delaying. Inside, we are scared individuals whose primary fear is being judged too harshly by those outside of us. That fear guides us and dominates our every move, burying us alive under expectations we put on ourselves, so that we never have to feel any shame of others, while we still feel it when we fail ourselves.

At the end of the day, we are all just incredibly scared...and that's okay.

CHAPTER 10

If You Scared, Say You Scared

I'm a Virgo. Now I'm not big into zodiacs and astrology so don't ask me for my chart and my moons because chances are I have no clue. What I have gathered, however is that Virgos all have a very similar tendency, and it is the meticulous nature by which we do things. Hence, many Virgos are known for their shared trait or self-professed perfectionism.

I've been laying the foreground for how much of a hindrance being a perfectionist can be, however in some cases that insatiable obsessive nature has pierced through to execution and presented itself as a benefit. Celebrities who have contributed their gifts and talents to the world who are Virgos include: Beyoncé, Keke Palmer, Adam Sandler, Kobe Bryant, Zendaya, Dave Chapelle, Salma Hayek, Stephen King, Idris Elba. Others come to mind such as Jennifer Hudson, Keanu Reeves, Jack Black, Taraji P. Henson, Bernie Sanders, Tyler Perry and even the late iconic Michael Jackson is a Virgo! I find it interesting that these trendsetters have this in common.

Now, despite how you feel personally about any of the aforementioned, I'm sure with a deep glance you can see how all of their careers have been earmarked with heavy cultural impact. Think about the hard work along with the massive milestones each of them has accomplished with their time here on earth. Multiple notable people on this short list have had the title of "the first person to…" or they fill out a "Top 5" list, and a few even on occasion, fall into the talks of the greatest of all time. Awards, honors, metals, and achievements can't even begin to encapsulate their measure of lasting life-altering work. Whether it was being in the spotlight since childhood, creating jobs and opportunities, diversifying to the point of becoming billionaires, transcending music, building studios, reshaping an entertainment sector, shifting the narrative of horror, or running for President! They are all perfectionists, and they pursued it relentlessly. Talent can only take you so far, and many of them have outworked the competition longer and harder.

> *"I'm chasing perfection."*
> —Kobe Bryant

The entire premise here is that if they chase perfection never to obtain it then you may land right at excellence! Virgos have a propensity to be highly detail oriented and analytical, have an obsessive work ethic, and will simply outwork anyone else to achieve what they want. Practicing at their craft repeatedly. Practice doesn't make perfect, but it does make permanent. So, when you show up, the job feels just like the rehearsal. In this way, they are the perfect perfectionists!

For me, this was eye-opening, especially when I watched Beyoncé in Act I and Act II of her stadium tours. I saw her meticulous nature, but I also witnessed sheer joy as she performed songs from over several decades alongside new genre-reclaiming hits. Every show didn't run perfectly, from mechanical malfunctions to inclement weather, missed stage marks, or wardrobe mishaps. However, throughout it all, she displayed excellence because she was doing what she loved in front of those who loved her, embracing the moment whether things were scary or unknown. She did it anyway with poise and class.

I wanted to be more practical with this advice to encourage you to aim for excellence instead of perfection. You'll notice how much more satisfying your results will become over time as you practice, and how much character you'll develop in the process. Joy comes as you grow more passionate about the beautifully imperfect nature of creating, especially as you get closer to your original vision with each attempt.

As stated in the opening of this topic of perfectionism, we must be consciously aware that our perfectionism is only bred out of our fear. We are scared. There is no other nice notable way to dress it up. We have genuine, debilitating, and in some cases valid fears the keep us in "the stuck" to never move forward. To think, you could have the same impact as Kobe or Beyoncé if you got out your own way. That would take a Mamba Mentality as Kobe called it. Perfectionism, however, arrests your mentality, making it mind-numbing, and offers you breadcrumbs of rewards to stay on the starved path. Yet, the real prize comes in feeling and facing the fears head-on. We have to state our fears out loud as perfectionists in order to know what we are dealing with. Most of our fears are tied to the same core feelings. So, allow me to lead the charge.

I am scared of…

1. Failure
2. Being judged
3. Not being good enough
4. Being rejected
5. Criticism
6. Not being liked
7. Being forgotten
8. Being embarrassed
9. Uncertainty
10. Being seen as incompetent

No matter how much inspiration, education, or motivation is out there, none of it will deny that these feelings of fear exist within. Our heart's work right in this very moment, my friend, is to acknowledge our fears. I want you to hold space for all the things you are scared of. Don't attempt to remove them so quickly from your orbit but understand where each comes from and their role in your life.

Your perfectionism is not the start; it usually is the means to an end. It is not the problem first, no, my friend, at some point, this was your solution. Going back to unearthing those developmental environments where we had to work to be loved and accepted, we created and conjured up a perfect existence as the answer. Your fears are not unjustified, but they are each a memory of a milestone in a time when you tried, and when your performance didn't pan out, you were left with a feeling of discomfort. All you ever wanted was to be accepted. All I ever wanted was to be embraced. We never wanted to be a perfect people pleaser; we just wanted to be loved for who we are. The cure and the blessing right here is to know that you don't have to ever be perfect to be seen, loved, valued, or recognized. You are enough... work or not.

I'm proud of you for facing these fears because you did what many couldn't. You learned how to adapt to survive so you wouldn't sink. Your subconscious mind did what it needed to do to protect you, and perhaps it served you for a time, but now the perfectionism has gotten out of control. That adaptation has turned into a harmful invasion of what you know to be true about yourself. The prison where your power is chained, locked away from your productivity, exists only in the depths of your own thoughts. So, as much as you learned how to adapt and survive through perfectionism, we must unlearn it to transcend and thrive by producing. You will make mistakes, you will let others down, and you will appear crazy while doing it. **Instead of running from it, embrace it!**

Reject Me Not

With close observation of some of the fear factors, I studied rejection longer than the others due to the nature that perfection stems from desiring acceptance and having to work for it. I found that rejection doesn't impact us all the same way, and it should be treated like most varying behavioral responses on a spectrum of intensities that diversify. Certain individuals will avoid rejection at any cost because it will produce physiological responses in them. It is unfair to tell someone to "stop being so sensitive" or to "shake it off" when this state of fearing rejection and, in some sense, being cautious about it, is their constant. I am not here to provide an amenable excuse for those who battle rejection, but to open up a dialogue and window of clarity to the varying degrees it may occupy.

Rejection Sensitivity Dysphoria (RSD), while not an official mental health condition, is an extreme emotional sensitivity and pain triggered by the perception that a person has been rejected or criticized by important people in their life. This can be linked to those with ADHD in some cases; however, this sensitivity may result in low self-esteem, shame, and overall withdrawal. It may also be triggered by a sense of falling short—failing to meet their own high standards or others' expectations.

If you have ever found yourself in a spiral once an ounce of rejection, critique, or even a perceived slight comes your way, you may be experiencing this, and chances are you've felt deeply alone. This could explain why a people-pleasing and perfectionism mechanism has kicked into gear when it comes to common tasks. I'm not a licensed doctor; I am just presenting common responses that we go through that make us feel like we are literally crazy.

It's okay to be afraid of rejection. I, too, have a healthy fear of rejection tied to a lingering thought of my own inadequacies that resides deep inside. Three common fears related to people-pleasing for me are being perceived as incompetent, receiving criticism, and being judged. I realized that to avoid feeling these things, I would try to create a perfect solution, situation, scenario, or shell where I could feel protected. For me, a sense of safety came from knowing I could potentially control how people responded based on what I put out or withhold. In this, I see how I found the breadcrumbs of my hidden reward at the expense of my deepest longing.

I'm scared, and I'm saying I'm scared. What we fear, which ties us to trying to be perfect, is not as scary, however, as what it will produce within us. Recall earlier, I spoke about how perfectionistic ideology and practicing acts as a mutation to help keep us protected. There are even more dangers that are cloaked beneath the umbrella that helps shield us from that fear.

Imposter Syndrome

What happens to us when the inevitable occurs and someone doesn't like your work or idea or compares it to something they deem as better? One of the most subtle things I have experienced in my own life is what happened when I took the risk to share myself and work with the world: if I am not accepted after putting in the sweat equity, I immediately transform. When I say I transform, I don't mean for the good to improve or just revert to meager people pleasing. No, I want to avoid any future hurt to my ego and exposure to my wounds and evade all those fears because I have now considered myself a failure. So, I transform into whatever new outfit is needed to keep me safe. Consider this: you may have completed the task, released the content, created the vision, and brought the product to market, yet you still find a corner to rest in with dissatisfaction, pretending you're fine, but knowing you are breaking inside.

My friends, this is called **Imposter Syndrome.** According to Merriam-Webster, Imposter Syndrome is a psychological condition characterized by persistent doubt concerning one's abilities or accomplishments, accompanied by the fear of being exposed as a fraud despite evidence of one's ongoing success.

Did you know that perfectionism is actually a form of imposter syndrome? That's right – it's an archetype Imposter syndrome. We are trying so hard not to be perceived as one thing that we create a false identity rooted in an impossible nature, and we

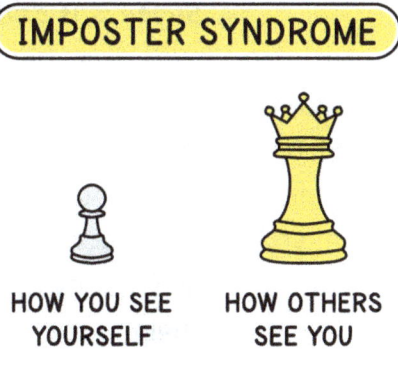

still end up being just as much of a fraud. The perfectionism born within us feeds this imposter syndrome. This is why I hate perfectionism. It is not a badge of honor; it is undoing all the hard work you have completed on yourself and your projects. You are creating a facade to hide your true self under so that your fears won't be exposed – this is an imposter. This perfectionist is not who you are; it's what you have become. There is no power in a perfection that doesn't exist; it is just an illusion.

From the onset of this journey, we walked through how we have all this potential that needs to be uncovered and how we desire more. We have put our pens to paper and charted out the lists and plans, gaining some momentum. Then we allow a form of perfectionism called procrastination to stop us dead in our tracks, and we fall back into overthinking, which kills the magic of it all. Eventually, after we sit there long enough, we get to the heart of why we won't start. And if we finally do, once we accomplish something, some of us wait, and a few moments later, the doubts, worry, and lack of self-worth creep in. This is tied directly to imposter syndrome.

Success is defined by doing.

You know, the odd thing about imposter syndrome is that it stems from doubting your own abilities despite you being a proven success, for fear of people thinking you aren't as good as what you have just accomplished. Yet, as a coping mechanism some of us (like myself) when we feel like we will be found out for not being good enough or "frauds", we transform into another type of imposter. Our authentic vulnerable self is buried somewhere deep under all the rubble and we can't tell one mask from the next so let me help identify them. I have already undressed that "The Perfectionist" is one of the imposter types where we get lost in the "how" and still disappointed when it is not flawless. What happens when that outfit isn't working anymore? Here are five other imposter types we may interchangeably wear:

1. **The Expert**

    They believe they need to be the lifelong learner and have all the answers. Constantly thriving on what they know and how much of it is readily available to regurgitate. Yet, they have massive feelings of shame and failure when they don't know something they believe they should.

2. **The Natural Genius**

    They believe that there should be ease and quickness with comprehension, so they are adverse to difficult tasks. They like to make things look easy, thrive on compliments of the like so typically if they can't grasp something the first time, they feel incompetent. It is their belief it should come naturally to them.

3. **The Soloist**

    They believe that they are the one designed to take on everything and can't ask anyone else for help. There is pride found for them in not asking for help even if they desperately need it, as that would be seen as a sign of weakness. As a result, they can take on too much at once to appear even stronger than they actually are.

4. **The Superhuman**

    They believe they have to do it all simultaneously and do it well. They take on as much as they can and turn down no request while trying to please everyone. If they drop the ball at one thing, they feel like a failure, and if their super elasticity in stretching themselves isn't validated, they may even become resentful.

5. **The Comedian**

    They believe they should stay behind the scenes and be more entertaining than vulnerable. They will downplay and minimize themselves before others have a chance to inspect or judge them. Additionally, they distract from any weaknesses with jokes, comedy, or sarcasm to deflect. Keeping things lighthearted helps them avoid the heavy feelings of uncertainty they experience.

When you suffer from imposter syndrome, you feel like you're not in control of your life; the character is. Thinking back to our procrastination chapter, you will begin to see parallels between the six types of procrastinators and the five types of imposters. All of this flows seamlessly as perfectionism is both a form of procrastination and a type of imposter syndrome.

What this comes down to is that how we really feel on the inside is not how we present ourselves on the outside. So, what we feel on the inside gets quieter and further from us as we present from the outside, and eventually those old limiting beliefs start to change our language. If you remain in the suit of an imposter long enough, you will start to talk like one, which is negative self-talk.

Have you ever caught yourself saying, "I can't do this until..." You are giving yourself permission to have an excuse because your imposter said it was okay. Let's have a healthy look at what impact your language has been having.

Can't vs Won't

These two words will often battle in our minds for heart territory to set up camp, and though they are often used interchangeably, they shouldn't.

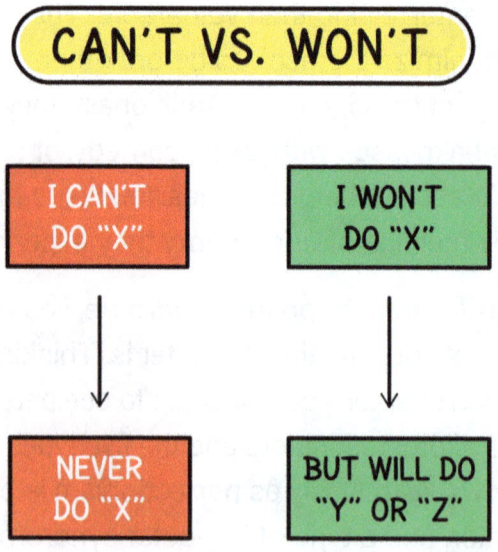

Can't means that one doesn't possess the power or ability to effect change. It may also refer to the environment or situation that is not conducive to change and is beyond our control to redirect. Can't means cannot, which is based on sets that can and will not change.

Won't means that one possesses the power or ability to make a change or act and invokes the choice not to do so. Albeit difficult or not, the party makes the conscious choice not to exert any effort in acting upon it. Won't means will not, which is based on your own unwillingness. This refers to your will and your choice to withhold something, according to how you exert your will and where.

Limiting beliefs often replace 'won't' with 'can't' to help us avoid taking responsibility for our actions. If someone truly believes they don't have the power to change or do anything, they will remain stuck in their development. But we began this discussion by emphasizing that it starts with you. Therefore, it cannot be true that you lack the power to act. It must be your environment or situation that's holding you back, right? Limiting beliefs don't just appear; they are the result of a once-limited mindset.

Director Christopher Nolan teamed up to cast one of my favorite leading actors, Leonardo DiCaprio, in a thought-provoking drama called *Inception*. The premise of the movie features DiCaprio as a sophisticated con artist who performs extraction, as he calls it, on the rich and powerful to steal their most valuable treasures and secrets. To make them reveal this information, he employs a technique called inception, where he embeds an idea deep into their subconscious while they sleep; however, he utilizes advanced technology to penetrate multiple layers of their subconscious. The subject experiences a dream within a dream within a dream. Then, he inserts himself into that dream as a friend acting in their best interest to get the target to betray their own self. Once they wake up in real life, they have no idea they were dreaming or that anyone was there with them, and by then, their next decisions are influenced by the subconscious planting of a seed by this master conman. Essentially, Leonardo DiCaprio waits for his target to fall asleep so he can invade their minds and plant seeds that lead them to betray themselves, both in words and actions.

Like the movie *Inception*, you are layers deep in your subconscious, and here is the environment you have built as you are wrestling with your ability.

1. The Invisible Crowd

A colosseum full of people that you have never met or engaged but you immediately have presuppositions for how they will respond to you and your ideas. This invisible crowd has enough tomatoes to throw on your stage and enough power to broadcast your failures as viral content. Your invisible crowd bears a striking resemblance to your past disappointments and mistakes. It feels and sounds a lot like your hard moments, the most adverse challenges, coupled with the pain and trauma you've endured. The invisible crowd is the judgment seat you have created for yourself that holds your fate in the balance. In your mind, it is the jury of your peers that is ready to cast the verdict. This isn't in any shape a fair trial because you never acted upon anything, yet here they are casting a guilty verdict over you.

Why do we give them so much power? Why is the invisible crowd not cheering and grasping for a seat at our table, eagerly waiting to join us? Why are they instead like piranhas looking for fresh meat to rip to shreds? The invisible crowd is a sea of rejection and judgment that we perpetuate to prepare for the death of our desires. It's all of our collective failure at once, with all their eyes upon us. That invisible crowd is neither a researched market, a target audience, nor a valid critique. It is a theatre full of our fears and failures, smiling back at us with tomatoes in hand and smear campaigns in full swing. You can walk off the stage of that invisible crowd.

And once we walk off the stage of the invisible crowd, we have one more created consciousness that keeps speaking to us.

2. The Silent Parent

The symbolism here is of a parent, but it can represent our guardian, mentor, or guide. This is the authority figure who was once in our lives and told us to go left or right. They taught us what to do and how to do it, and we are still trying to make them proud. In some cases, we may not have had that person present in real time, and we've tried to make up actions to earn their approval since we blame ourselves for their absence. Whatever the case, we want this person or these people to feel like we did the right thing and that we have value and merit. The silent parent is often the loudest voice in the environment we created.

The reason they are a silent parent/authority is that they never really say much of anything, but you can infer what they think or feel. This is the voice that can make you second-guess yourself every time you are about to execute and return right after you do. This silent authority can grow louder when risk is involved, telling you not to embarrass yourself or to think carefully first. The silent parent doesn't have to say a word, just the look or body posturing will put you on pause. Can you imagine sitting in front of your invisible crowd of fears and failures, and your silent parent is in the audience, looking at you for perfection and precision?

You may constantly hear these looping phrases in your mind from this type of silent parent:

- *"Make sure you do it right."*
- *"How is that ever going to work?"*
- *"I wouldn't do that if I were you..."*

The silent parent can be a ringing menace in our subconscious. Perhaps our parents, mentors, or authorities never told us any of these things. In our minds, we have to prove that we have things under control. We have to show all the work and how we know for sure that it will be a winner, so some of us get dressed up here as the expert imposer. The environment we set on the stage for us to perform our biggest ideas is one filled with our critics.

What we succumb to is not the act of unpacking and breaking down what these voices and inhibitions are, but we yield to fortified limiting beliefs as immutable. They cannot be questioned or overruled, and they are part of the permanence of the prisons in which our creativity resides. The silent parent and the invisible crowd were created as the environment of our stage in our minds.

But how does all this information about our fears, imposter syndrome, and created audiences relate to who we have become today? Let's run down the list of our three P's on how this all will impact the grand show!

Planning

Are all the plans in place for our moment? The reason we come up with plans and more plans is not merely for our own organization and clarity. In part, it is for us to make sure our invisible crowd knows we have a way forward. The overplanning was for the silent parent who sits in disapproval, and we have to convince them that this time we've struck gold. The plans are made and revised to answer every question unasked and every judgment unpassed. This is how we soothe the silent parent and invisible crowd, or so we think…

Procrastinating

The stage is calling us, and it's showtime in five minutes, but we never show up. Instead, since this is our show, we make up an excuse for a delay and we use all the tools. We throw in words like "I can't," surrendering our power and abilities to logical fallacies. We engrain that into our minds and blame it on the invisible crowd. "I can't come out with this now because the audience I'm looking to reach doesn't have this or expects that." The invisible crowd is an audience with a blood thirst and will never have enough fresh meat to chew on. All this planning and procrastinating is for them. In our minds, we're thinking about them and that's why we didn't start. We have abandoned the best version of ourselves, and we lay under the guillotine of guilt of our worst inner critics.

Perfectionist

We are supposed to be on stage in two minutes, but it wouldn't hurt to go over it behind the scenes one more time. When the final moment comes—when we're supposed to step into the light of the destiny that awaits us—we become perfectionists. We re-examine every line, every detail, and each word, and we overhaul what we have prepared. It can be better; it must be better; it has to be better! What will the authority I've been trying my whole life to validate my worth think if everything isn't perfect? What if I perform and present, and it isn't pleasing? It has to be perfect. I'll take as much time as I need to improve my chances of success.

I'm painting the scene, but in real time, all of this is happening in the recesses of your mind. We consume more knowledge, add it to our plans, and push out deadlines further as we go over things once again with a fine-tooth comb. Whenever someone asks about all that potential we have, we shy away with small plates. We abandon the responsibility of starting with ourselves because we believe we have more to deliver within ourselves. Instead, we don't perform; we reduce ourselves to the environment of the audiences we've created. We shift from one state of anxiety to another, fearing judgment and rejection.

Now, when someone asks about what you have going on, you utter those words, "I was thinking about..." That's everything you've learned in this book so far summed up, only now you understand the WHY behind what has been happening.

You've been thinking so long that you are unsure where to even start when you share. You have muffled your own voice and masked your insecurities so well that, at this point, you are unsure what you genuinely feel versus what you project. Do you feel beat up after all this? I'm sorry, but this is the beating that your authentic self has been taking behind the curtain. It's time to be free of fear. Do it anyway my friend…Just do it!

CHAPTER 11

Progress Over Perfection

"Perfection is a roadblock to progress."
—Unknown

This chapter will discuss what is called the ideation stage. The ideation stage is a beautiful place to be, and it is the birthplace of creativity. Before you put down all the plans and counted all the risks, there was unrelenting creativity and tenacity that formed whole worlds in your mind. There was no stopping you there. Many of us wish we could stay there and be in a constant self-induced think-tank while churning out new ideas and inventions as worthwhile contributions. The best way to manifest all that you see within, is to just let it out of its cage. You have given it enough thought and you don't need any more time to compile additional reasons as to why you shouldn't start right where you are.

Progress always wins because, along the endless road to perfection, you will, in fact, become the perfect version of yourself. That's the secret no one actually tells you. The journey of the road to perfection is long and difficult. It is soiled with disappointments and defeat. The road has hanging fruit in the form of bitter lessons and pungent growth. The reward, however, is not perfection but the pursuit of it despite our imperfections. The truest gift is the privilege to be on the road. It takes tenacity to start anything. I just need you to start. Start walking. The situation may look overwhelming, and you might even feel helpless or not know what to do with everything in your heart, but it's beating out of your chest.

Done > Perfect

I am a sucker for a good Denzel flick, and I may succumb to an occasional impersonation from time to time. In the movie *John Q*, starring Denzel Washington, he portrays a small-town father whose son is diagnosed with an enlarged heart and who finds out he is unable to receive a transplant because HMO insurance will not cover it. John ends up selling all his belongings to help pay for his son's transplant, but it still wasn't enough. The climax of the movie was when his wife frantically pleaded with him to find any way to fix the problem and get the transplant for their son. She then yells to him over the phone, "Do you hear me, John? Do something!"

That is what I'm saying to you, my friend. We have been crippled by our own fear, doubt, and excuses for too long. It doesn't matter where you are, how it looks, or what you feel.

Not tomorrow, right now. You must do something.

In full transparency, it is 4:02 AM in Denver, Colorado, and I am writing this section of the book to you in a dark hotel room with my face dimly lit by the backlight of my computer monitor.

This is my "DO SOMETHING" moment! Creating this book in its most raw form is the moment I chose progress over perfection. I chose to start with myself and make this happen because I no longer want to be a planning procrastinating perfectionist. I am full of disgusting potential and healthy education.

Shouldn't it be your time? (Rhetorical question) Release that massive idea to create a huge footprint on the earth. Any progress whatsoever into the outside world is better than your unmet template for perfection. Start big or small, but just start. **Do it in pain, do it distant, do it ugly, do it angry but do it!**

When I was 22, I was the founding Director of a non-profit focused on mobilizing young adults for community volunteerism and activism. We were all struggling and working hard with little to no funds or support. I came across a startup boot camp in New York called 'Do Something.' How fitting, right? They hosted workshops and awarded grants to young social entrepreneurs under 25 years old. I selected ten of my staff and volunteers who met the criteria, and we traveled from Philadelphia to New York City on the Megabus, wearing our branded apparel. We arrived at the conference ready to learn and be inspired by other young trailblazers and innovators. Something remarkable happened that day: as we participated in workshops and networked, we got uncomfortable. We stepped out of our comfort zone in Philly and ventured into unfamiliar territory to make our presence known. It was thrilling to see us as passionate young urban youth led by a similarly young and zealous director. My organization needed a boost of inspiration and support to keep moving forward, and I took a bold step to address the issue.

Through this, I learned that **all the planning will pay off if you stop procrastinating and allow the journey to perfect you in the process.**

You should know that, prior to our team's visit to New York, I would rigorously train staff and volunteers to articulate our mission statement. I set up speed-dating style sessions where each person would explain our mission and give a uniform elevator pitch. I invested money into professional development and rented out facilities to enrich unpaid volunteers. Everyone wore the same shirt with the same colors and our mission statement on the back. Then we stumbled upon the *Do Something* bootcamp, and they featured an activity that would allow us to show off our prowess. All our planning and perfecting for "one day" had come out of my action to make it today.

While somewhat intimidated amidst competing orgs that seemed so much more polished than ours, an opportunity arose. There was a competition that would award one with a $500 seed grant for whomever could best pitch their mission statement. My eyes lit up! Here we are all the way from Philly, amped up, fully uniformed and we prepared for this! When they called my name, I got the team ready, we stood in the middle of the room and boldly recited our mission statement. I closed it with my introduction and vision all under one minute. As a result, we went home recipients of our first ever seed grant from a group that was all about empowering young people who were committed to social change.

My challenge to you right now is to launch something into real time. I don't care if its securing a name of a website, creating content right where you are, putting the down payment for your investment in an account, filing legal entity paperwork, or releasing graphic imagery saying coming soon. I want you to do something now! It needs to be public, and it needs to happen now. Progress outside of your blueprints and in a live audience in real-time is the only way we get out of our own way. That audience you created does not exist – remember, **no one** but you matter in this moment of starting. The real world needs to know that you are stepping out of your comfort zone and into the mud. You need to be handcuffed to your future success, and the only way to do that is by breaking the laws of your limiting beliefs and allowing the beauty of action taken to arrest you! The boot camp was an opportunity for me to act, and it paid off with a reward. My hope is that this book will serve as your ignition to take action on your one thing right away for your benefit.

My story was from my twenties, and while the social landscape has changed significantly despite the algorithms, the barriers to entry, or the 8 billion other people that exist, you are still very special. Commit this to memory:

The world doesn't want the perfect version of you, they need the real version of you—your authentic self showing up, unashamed despite adversity, while ever learning and always improving.

That's the secret sauce. Don't try to fit into this grid, because you are already crafted to be different. Repetition of the same old ideas is boring and stale. Allow your innovation to align with your vision and create something beautiful from all that you are today.

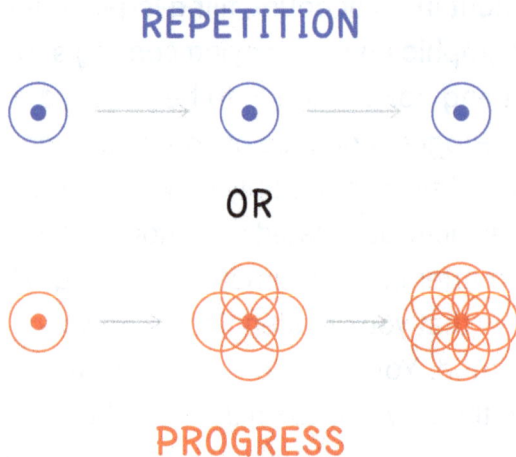

Progress looks different for everyone in this age, but they all have to start doing something. Look at the power of overnight successes and celebrities in the rise of TikTok. I have watched 16–22-year-olds become brand ambassadors, paid partners, and full-blown celebrities online. Amassing a following and being rewarded for making content that was true to them. Some of them decided to create their own makeup tutorials, while others shared their daily rants and unique perspectives. Some have made comedic content, others have started trends, and many have started livestreaming or playing games. Still others offer health & balanced advice. They have become voices and faces to an audience that needed representation, and as a result, the followers come flocking. The comments, the reshares, the engagement, it catches like a wildfire that is never quenched, and once that ball starts rolling, the momentum is irreversible. Before you know it, what started on one platform as TikTok is being reposted on Facebook, X (formerly Twitter), YouTube, and Instagram Reels. How did all this happen?

Some kid with a dream or out of boredom opened their phone every day with their ring light camera, wherever they were, and made their dreams come true by being consistent. Chances are they didn't have some elaborate content strategy, a marketing plan, or own anything other than their phone and a tripod. The secret sauce was all that they needed. The brands come knocking, with paid partnerships, sponsored deals, and free swag. It comes because that dreamer became a doer, and their impact created influence, and influence turns into dollars from big brands that aren't as connected to a core audience of consumers. Look at how the pipeline to profit started with being the most authentic version of themselves and just showing up every single day. Maybe you don't know it yet because we are just used to looking at finished products, but that is how it's done my friend!

Consistency and commitment mixed with discipline and determination. We all start somewhere, and it doesn't always look polished when we do. However, for all the ones out there that like to make it look good while you are at it that's still possible.

Examine the Swan

People often marvel at the elegance and grace of the swan. They admire its smooth wings and long, curved neck as it glides across the water with an almost angelic presence. The swan has a large wingspan of about 6 to 10 feet, but its

THE CALM WE SEE

THE EFFORT WE DON'T SEE

wings stay tucked in as it drifts through the water. From an outsider's perspective, the swan seems completely calm, but there's more going on beneath the surface. When you look below the water, the swan's feet are frantically paddling, almost panicked, and on the verge of drowning. The effort underwater isn't visible to the observer, but it's essential for keeping the bird afloat and moving from one place to another. While onlookers admire the swan's serene appearance above, it's fighting desperately underneath. That's the process and the journey. If you want to present yourself like the swan, go ahead—kick, paddle, work hard, and push toward your goals while maintaining a calm demeanor to be admired. It's possible, but only through hard work and self-awareness.

Be the Swan

Take Pride in It

We cannot think that we are supposed to be validated for what we want to do; you actually have to do it. We need motion, my friend; otherwise, what can you take pride in? I'd like to submit that we have been taking in ego more than pride this entire time we've been stuck. Two more words that are used interchangeably yet don't equate to the same definition. We may have been protecting the Ego this entire time while sacrificing the Pride that comes as the prize of work produced.

Ego is your self-perception and how you view yourself, which can often lead to arrogance, resentment, bitterness, or a lack of compassion.

Pride is an emotion that you get from a sense of accomplishment. This is what you feel when you have a level of self-satisfaction, and it can be derived from others or oneself.

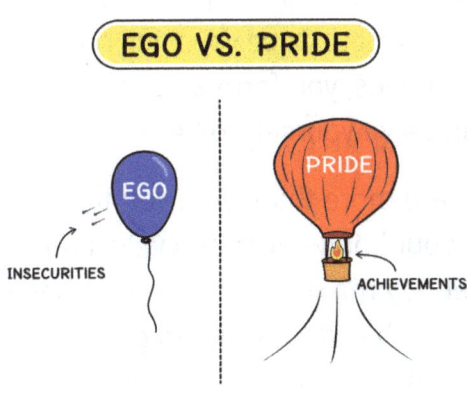

You can't take pride in anything until you have created something. Therefore, do the work to create something. The fuel to keep you rising is different when you do.

Whether you are religious or not, I believe this is a spiritual principle. The spirit within all men and women is something I see as eternal and everlasting. It is the power we all hold and harness to create. Spirit within us speaks to our ingenuity, creativity, and drives our passion, serving as the source of our purpose. It is in my spirit that I can take pride in my work, in the success of others, or in my contributions to society. Spirit is divine, and it has the ability to create and be harmonious with everything it touches, which is why I believe I can never fail at my purpose.

I believe, however, the soul of a person is equated with the mind. Soul is where we derive our principles, values, morals, logic, beliefs, and thought patterns. It is where our reality and logic live. We don't dream from the mind/soul, we dream from the spirit. Imagination occurs on a deep spiritual level, and it cannot be eradicated or destroyed. However, the soul is what guides our everyday lives. It is the rudder that helps us steer risk and ensure we are doing what's in our best interests. Your mindset is an integral part of your soul, and that is why there is a battle for your soul. Whoever controls the mind controls the body. The difficulty with your mind/soul is that it is easily influenced and swayed by distractions if exposed to certain programming for a prolonged period. Once you latch onto core beliefs, limitations, and ideologies, you form an ego around it because this is who you perceive yourself to be.

I want to suggest that you are more than what you think you know. Clear your mind, let your imagination run wild, and see how much pride you'll feel. Try making no decisions based on logic and observe how much further you can go. There is freedom in exploring the unknown and allowing the spirit within you to run free, simply creating. This is your true self. Align your spirit with new mindsets so your soul is in harmony, and then your body can act it out. Mankind is body, soul, and spirit. Be in alignment and watch how you will create magic in the world.

This will take work; you don't just fall into being a creator of your own world. People often talk about manifesting it, speaking things into existence, aligning with the universe, or praying and relying on God. Whatever your take on it is, just remember to return to the source and be intentional with what you want out of the encounter.

Many will tell you this is a mindset shift. If you spend enough time with wealthy and powerful people, they will likely discuss the changes in their mindset. This is intentional work in order to grow to the highest versions of ourselves, where we see the impossible as possible, we need to adopt a growth mindset. The perfectionist, with all their ego and limitations, has a fixed mindset. They are in a box of their own making and can only see as far as their hand can touch or their currently trapped mind can grasp.

Allow me to show you the differences between a growth mindset and a fixed mindset and I want you to see if you can spot some of the fears of the perfectionists and their behavior patterns.

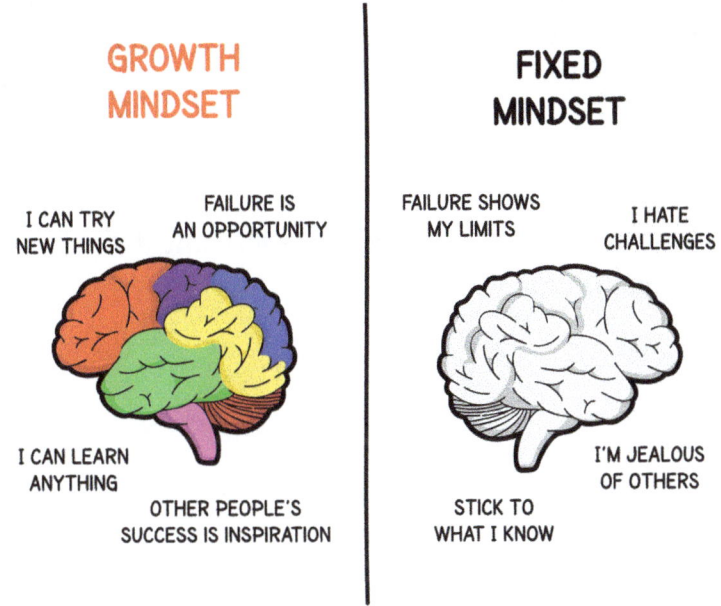

The perfectionist will seldom admit this, but they have a fixed mindset, which is why they believe they have the power to make something perfect before they produce it. The reasoning behind their actions has already been established, and this culminates in hardening them into a stubborn, fixed mindset. All the behaviors that emit out of that are only a byproduct of a mind that needs to be renewed. It's crucial to know that they don't want to operate this way, but they need to feel a sense of accomplishment. What comes instead is a sense of falsified pride for their inactivity, as they actually feed their ego through different forms of imposters, all starting with a mindset that craves growth.

Progress over perfection means we have to help you move beyond The Stuck. The term "The Stuck" refers to individuals who are in a loop, often caused by their perfectionism. The stuck is where spirits go to be muzzled, and imaginations turn into impossibility. Being stuck in this way usually means that you are so overwhelmed that your behavior displays a lack of action, and the mindset shows a lack of or a stuck belief system. No forward movement or progress can occur from this point.

Getting unstuck is simple once you realize one thing: **You can't control everything.**

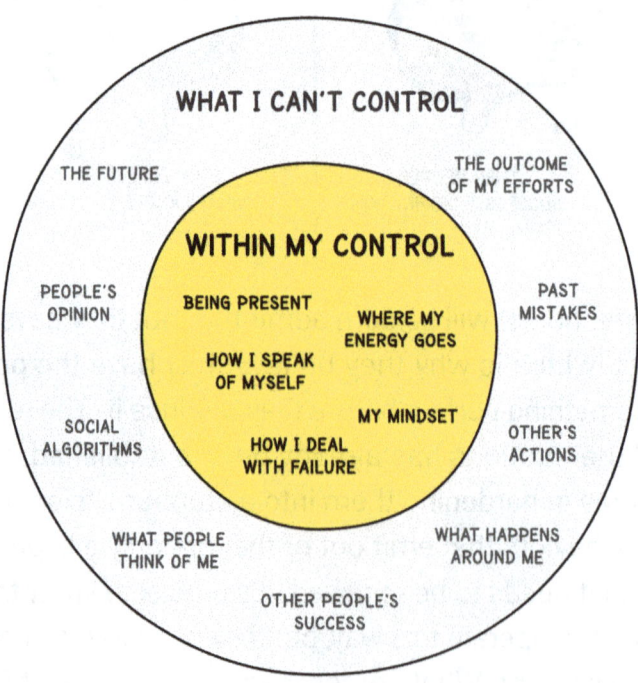

Your focus should be on everything inside your control instead of outside of it. Create a sphere for yourself and realize that no one holds the keys to your destiny unless they are within your sphere. Only you can control what you put out. At the same time, I need you to take your hands off the wheel of other people's lives, expectations, and accomplishments. You have no power to determine their mindsets or feedback. The harsh reality is you can't predict or define how the world and market will respond once you create what you've spent years working on. What you can do to achieve a level of success that brings you true pride is to focus on what you can control. That's how you get unstuck and do this imperfectly while staying true to yourself.

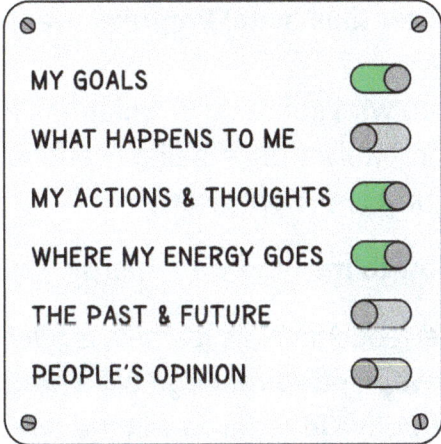

Focus on your:

- Attitude
- Alignment of energy
- Reactions

- Energy output
- Social engagement
- Boundaries
- Self-Talk
- Times for rest and rejuvenation
- Ability to ask for help

Your sole responsibility to allow space for your dreams, ambitions, and passions to thrive is to get the hell out of the way! The best way to remove yourself is to provide yourself with the utmost care, and once you release it from your hand, return to yourself and celebrate your small wins. Continue this process until it becomes second nature or muscle memory. The step-by-step nature is going to perfect you, but you have to know that practice doesn't make perfect, it makes permanent.

Done is better than none! Progress over Perfection!

I will provide you with some quick solutions to this, because I know you're probably tired of being overwhelmed and need help with your problem, right? Perfect.

- **Know how to manage your energy**

    Since perfectionism, as learned, is a form of procrastination, we need to manage our energy output to be most effective in order to win the day and defeat the battle within. Follow your flow:

ENERGY OUTPUT PROTOCOL

LOW ENERGY DAY

- BE KIND TO YOURSELF
- GIVE YOURSELF PERMISSION TO REST
- REMEMBER IT WON'T FEEL LIKE THIS EVERYDAY
- PRIORITIZE YOUR SELF-CARE

MEDIUM ENERGY DAY

- TAKE A SHOWER
- MAKE A LIST OF THINGS YOU NEED TO DO
- TACKLE THE SMALLEST/QUICKEST TASKS
- TAKE A SHORT WALK AND RECONNECT WITH YOURSELF

HIGH ENERGY DAY

- MAKE A TO-DO LIST
- START WITH THE BIGGER TASKS
- MOVE YOUR BODY
- JOURNAL ABOUT YOUR DAY
- TAKE CARE OF YOURSELF

- **Revisit the two-minute rule to continue to get unstuck**

    The two-minute rule states that if a task can be done in two minutes, it should be done immediately and then move on. This will counteract your procrastination and prevent perfectionism from taking hold.
    If you let that task sit, you will find a way to poke holes in it, making it larger than necessary, and it will take longer. Don't turn a bullet point into a billboard. Do it in two minutes or less and celebrate the small win.

- **Embrace the mindset of I'm ready already**

    You should remind yourself daily to be skeptical of what you think you know. None of us knows everything, and if we are always learning, then there is always room for improvement. That does not mean we do not act. We are ready to get started.

The challenge here is to lovingly admit to yourself that I don't know everything, yet I am willing to continue elevating my learning, all while implementing what I do know.

The same is true for your perfectionism. Maintain your high standards but pursue them as you go. Don't wait, and don't impose unrealistic ideals on the entire project you're working on; otherwise, failure will result from producing nothing. You don't control time, and it will continue to pass. However, you do control your actions or inaction within the framework of time. You are more than ready. Give yourself grace because it creates space. What will you do now? Something…one thing… nothing? This is the part you control.

CHAPTER 12

You Are Unstoppable

I'd like to begin this chapter with a story...

One early morning, around 1 AM, I was restless and found myself swirling with a myriad of my imagination, visions, and ideas. Some of them I had already acted on and wanted to build out and advance, while others were mere musings. My brain became overstimulated as I struggled with purpose, trying to figure out how all my skills, passions, and multidisciplinary interests were interconnected. I felt isolated, lonely, even a bit manic, and in a state where I knew no one would truly understand me. I stayed up that morning, verbally processing this to myself until it all clicked, and by 3 AM, I had written it down. I thought to myself, "Ok great, it's out of my head and now back into planning mode...Here I go following my same old cycle."

I assumed I was simply doing what I always did until there was a spark that thrust me in a different direction, and my excitement drove me to a decision. I scoured the internet and bought a plane ticket across the country to book a four-day stay. I knew absolutely nothing about the place I was flying to, not even any landmarks or sites, and there was no one there. I didn't have the money allocated for a vacation or an itinerary – I just booked it. One ticket to Denver, Colorado. It seems impulsive, right? Why did I do that? It was because in that moment I knew then what you know now, which is that I will be the cause of my own demise if I stay in a cannibalistic cycle of rinse and repeat. Progress requires you to attach your thinking to doing. I knew I needed to accompany my great potential and plans with some radical action to induce immediate progress that would birth future success.

Scheduling the flight and hotel forced me to do what I had loudly proclaimed concerning the creation of a manuscript, yet this book in particular would be just one aspect of where I was headed. You see, momentum had already been working in my favor because I had been doing some pretty off the wall things that kept me fueled to keep going. Just two weeks prior to arranging this trip to write a book, I had purchased a separate ticket to a social event of entrepreneurs, took a paid course from the host, and made sure it was in a different city. When I had arrived at the venue in Atlanta I networked, flushed out ideas, built my confidence and it yielded even more than I expected in outcomes. Upon returning from that trip and before hopping on the plane to Colorado to lockdown for the manuscript writing session, I began reciting a phrase over and over:

You are unstoppable.

The moment you make a little progress and do something publicly, you become unstoppable. My friend, listen to me— you're an unstoppable force. Stop just telling people about your ideas and start showing them what you're doing and when it will be finished. When I booked my trip to Colorado, I told all my closest friends I was flying to Denver to write and finish my book. Guess who looks like a fool and a bigger failure when returning to the East Coast with unfinished work? This guy! I had to attach myself to expectations of success to motivate myself. I hijacked my brain and challenged my perfectionist side in a good way, while also giving it a deadline. What are you willing to do?

You want to know what I think? I think you are afraid of how unstoppable you will become. Once you pick up speed and start making progress, you will not be stopped. Envision yourself with that ego in check, fear in the back seat, as you accomplish micro goals and do it scared and imperfect while employing tactics of the successful, as you remember it all starts with you. That's an unstoppable individual. Think back to that Eisenhower matrix. What is most urgent and important here – your launch and entrance into your goals. The only thing you need to be sharing is deadlines and celebrating milestones. There is nothing else to talk about.

You are unstoppable, but that means that when your dream is driving its headed towards a destination with a deadline and the final stop is success. Being unstoppable in this way means you don't have time or energy to redirect to others to see who is doing what. You're conserving and directing energy at the highest points to the most important items in order to maximize your efficiency. The unstoppable version of you sacrifices the distractions for the destination. Expect the speed bumps, appreciate the delays, yield, when necessary, but they keep fucking going.

On my journey to write my self-published book years ago as a bit of trial and error, I developed a mantra to keep me focused called **P.T.P.**, which was an exponential acronym that stood for:

Protect the Purpose
Preserve the Purity
Pursue the Plan

As you can tell between the title of this work and that mantra, I clearly have a thing for alliteration with P's. I would recite P.T.P. to myself anytime I wanted to refocus on being action-oriented and obtaining my goals. This is the moment you realize you are the priority, and you must keep secure what matters most. This notion of being unstoppable means nothing, and no one will get in the way of you seeing your imagination come to manifestation. Birthing what is inside to live freely on the outside is the main priority.

Now, in having this mindset, you may be afraid to leave your friends behind. I was too when I needed to ascend. It's a real and present thing when your company and some friendships may not grow you or stretch you anymore. Intellectually you seem to be on another plane. Looking to the future with great vision and learning all there is to know about what you want to invest yourself in. You become unstoppable. That includes not having any time to stop for friends who are not on board with the vision. If they can't assist you where you are going or provide honest, informed critique and accountability, you need to go on without them. I am not telling you to abandon your friends, I am telling you, don't abandon your heart's mission for them. That is a form of self-betrayal.

This is where the rubber meets the road for some of you. All those quotes and retweets about "everybody can't go with you," and yet here you are trying to load extra unnecessary cargo onto your journey. This isn't about them; it's about you, and it starts with you. Don't worry if we do it correctly; it will end with them. They will never truly benefit from understanding and loving the real you if you constantly forfeit parts of yourself and your purpose. Whether you succeed or fail, it will be you who is responsible, so don't do yourself a disservice by inviting everyone in who can't see where you're headed. Vision is important, and if my inner circle can't see the big picture, why would I give them a brush to help touch up the canvas? The final picture will always be off if I do that and drag them through my process. This isn't a damn paint and sip; we are working on a masterpiece here, and I need you sober!

Instead, take a moment to step away and unleash your creativity, using the genius of the PTP mantra to develop the final portrait. Same canvas, different process. Yes, you're unstoppable once you begin, but you often get stopped if you start with the wrong things. Drop the dead weight before you begin the journey. You don't have to be mean; just start speaking the truth about yourself out loud.

Start writing periodically on your social media "I am unstoppable" with no context, no fluff, no pictures of yourself. Just the phrase. It's not only a public affirmation, but it's a challenging declaration, even to yourself, as to how you take up space in a room. You are letting everyone know publicly what you know about yourself privately, even if you don't always fully believe it in the moment. That level of confidence does a few things for you. It will tie you to the expectation of your excellence.

Perfectionism done right has you focused on excellence as your true intent. Well, go tell the outside you're unstoppable because their next natural response will be "oh yeah, prove it!" That's when you get to shine and execute at the high level you've been waiting to act on.

People will naturally reposition themselves around how they engage with you when you walk in that level of confidence. It's not boastful or arrogant – you really are unstoppable. You will get those who poke fun in your comments, mimic you in person, or make a joke and make light of your posts. The invisible crowd just became visible. Respond to those real people with real action. Keep affirming publicly, "I am unstoppable," while working tirelessly and silently in the background and knocking out your goals. Be silent about what matters most and be loud about your presence alone.

> **Do not sacrifice your soul's purpose for a sole person – EVER.**

Just talk your shit. To yourself. To your friends. To whoever is listening. Talk it and talk it heavy. Confidence is attractive. If you don't believe in yourself, why should anyone else? I challenge all my friends who are doing great things to talk and walk heavy! When you come into the room, represent yourself well with titles, your passion, and an inspiring pitch. Break that small plate and show off!

When I was in early adulthood, I was still deeply into the indie music scene of writing and recording as a blooming performing rap artist, and it always blew my mind at all my peers around me who thought they would get big from it. These were very ambitious creatives who modeled their styles after their favorite icons and notarized artists, and they were looking for their place in it all. There were some talented people who naturally just had what it took. They had that disgusting potential you couldn't help but notice. I watched them appear to be on the path to being unstoppable, but there was a missing component somewhere.

They walked and talked heavily, for sure; however, since they were smelling themselves in a positive light, many had also adopted a mindset that things would come easily to them. So, with that adaptation, they didn't walk far or for too long. In our studies, they would be considered the dreamer version of a procrastinator.

Since they were naturally talented, they relied solely on that. But you know the saying, "Hard work always beats talent when talent doesn't work hard." I would encounter far less skilled musicians and artists going harder every single day for themselves. As organized as I was as a rapper back then, I would observe these artists study the craft, seek help about publishing and royalties, and want to know the business of building a brand behind the music.

In being unstoppable, I was acutely aware that regardless of the competition, the consistent one wins.

Consistency Always Wins

Sitting back, it was those people who grew on me and I came to support because of one thing – Consistency. It wins every single time. You don't have to make a big splash when you first step out; just be consistent and never stop. Your longevity and relentlessness will help you overcome many of the basic hurdles that others would face. Develop a strategic mindset that is solely focused on achieving results. Whatever mishaps or obstacles come up in the way, we run it over and learn from them to know how to pivot or maneuver, because we are stoppable. When your motor is in gear to move forward, along with the acceleration not being based on other people's opinions or approval, you **will** become unstoppable. You owe this to yourself.

Calvin Broadus Jr. who we know as Snoop Dogg, has been unstoppable since his days growing up in Long Beach. He started in church and athletics, but by sixth grade his gift for music was already drawing crowds. Calvin was unstoppable.

Raised by a single mother, he faced jail time and the pull of the streets. Instead of letting those setbacks and his environment define him, he turned them into his fuel. Recording with his cousins Nate Dogg and Warren G, he kept pushing until a tape landed in the hands of Dr. Dre. His upbringing was far from perfect, but his style, talent, and authenticity carried him forward. He was unstoppable.

From there, he signed to Death Row Records and released *Doggystyle*, an album that launched him into hip-hop history with his West Coast G-Funk swag. Even when facing a murder trial for which he was acquitted, he turned that defining moment into art, releasing his *Murder Was the Case* song and proving once again that he would not be stopped.

When Tupac was killed and Death Row Records began to collapse, Snoop could have faded away. His contract was terrible, his circle was breaking apart, and his next project didn't hit as hard. That would have been enough for most people to quit. Instead, he founded his own label, learned the business, and continued to push forward. Snoop was and is unstoppable.

And here's the point: regardless of how you feel about him, we see that his nature is rooted in being consistent with his craft and calling. Fast forward a few years, and Snoop is one of the most successful and recognizable entertainers in the world. He has sold millions of albums and built a career that reaches far beyond music. He has created businesses, invested wisely early on companies like Klarna and Reddit, and built an empire that includes cannabis ventures and alcohol brands. He runs his own youth football league and is still married to his wife after decades from when he first got signed! Most recently, he was selected as the face of the 2024 Olympics. None of this would have happened if he had waited for the perfect moment or given up folded, waiting for the right time. Remember he signed to Death Row Records? He now owns it.

He stayed consistent, committed, and focused, which is why he is unstoppable. And if you choose consistency over your 3-P problem, so are you. There is no such thing as an overnight success. There will be daily failures, momentary struggles, life lessons, and growth opportunities. However, when met with the perseverance to endure you will win.

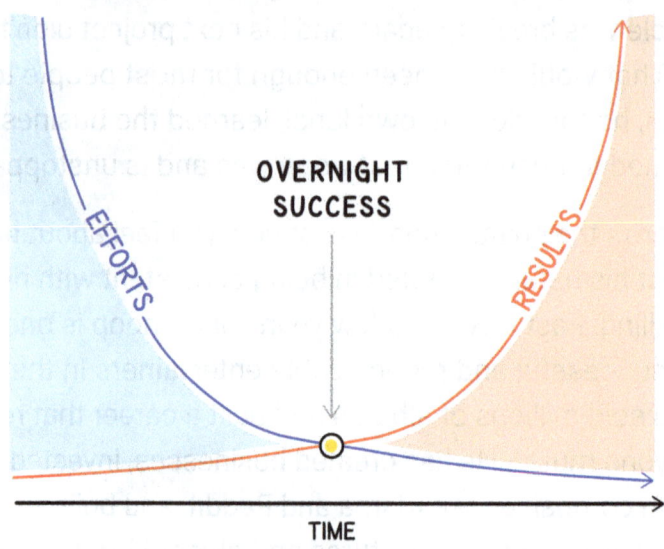

Consistent Commitment beats the Planned Procrastinating Perfectionism every single time.

Vision Becomes Mission

I want to bring you a little closer because I've been calling you my friend this entire time, so let me treat you as such by sharing a bit more about myself. When my divorce process began in the fall of 2020 and wasn't finalized until January 2022, I experienced a rapid transformation within myself. I had to confront deep, raw emotions, explore the dark corners of my soul, and face my shadows. I fought with the beliefs I told myself so that the truth of who I am could become my guiding light during times of distress or discouragement. Unlearning has become my greatest form of learning, shaping me into the person I am today. I created a vision board instead of written plans because I needed a visual representation of what I wanted for myself. How you speak to yourself is important, but how you see yourself and what you envision for your future are just as vital. They reveal your determination about your self-worth and what you believe you deserve. That's why, on August 14, 2022, I chose to make a vision board.

This practice proved to be incredibly powerful for me, especially when I did it alone. I didn't need to be at some New Year's Eve party with a bunch of friends, champagne, and magazines. My plans cover the whole apartment I'm living in, and I don't need any more motivation to pursue them. This was a personal journey. I needed to understand who I was, who I was talking to, who I was becoming, and how I saw myself. I needed to visualize where I wanted to be and what it looked like. It doesn't matter how silly, vague, or huge it might seem to others—what mattered was that I knew it was in my inner vision, and then I could bring it into my outer view. Only then could I pursue it as my mission, and once it's in my sights, that's what would make me unstoppable.

Walk with me as I break down some of this board to bring you closer to my heart. I placed images of my younger self on diagonal corners because my inner child had been screaming to be released after years of being buried due to misplacement, suppressed authenticity, and growing up trying to identify with others while navigating a childhood narcissistic father wound. I needed that young Dante to shine brightly again, the one who was there before I created masks to fit in and be palatable. I put on small things like contacts because I wore glasses and was too scared to ever try contacts to return me back to my original look. Also, I added a chart of excellent credit because mine has always been fair or below since I became an adult due to mismanagement which limited financial opportunities for me early on.

There were fun images of palm trees, beautiful beaches, and meditation. These are moments I longed for because I wanted to relocate to California and experience Zen meditation and peace. Being in the beauty of nature, amidst a new city, and surrounded by some of the best sands I've seen in the States. Labels like "make new traditions" and "freedom" were everywhere because I was determined to break the cycle of repetition passed down to me that made me feel I could only live one way and follow my family or friends. Starting new traditions, like financial literacy, was very important to me. To reinforce this, I placed a chart of boundaries at the bottom to help keep that freedom intact once I achieved it.

The characters on the bottom left of my board are from either shows or movies, and all but one of them are fictional. The one at the top that is non-fictional is Clarence Avant – the black godfather, a fixer, and background mover and shaker in the entertainment industry. His life and legacy are quite profound, and I saw myself in his motives as he quietly helped forge and create other living legends. He is a legend in the making by creating legends – what a legacy.

You would have to watch the shows and the movie to understand the other characters fully, but here is a brief snippet I took from each of them:

Raymond Reddington of *The Blacklist* is witty, savvy, and deeply connected to powerful circles. Though a fugitive, his deeper motive is to do good, and he uses his network to help a young FBI agent rise while staying close to the only family he has left, secretly, and keeping his most vulnerable parts concealed.

Olivia Pope of *'Scandal'* is a stylish and commanding D.C. fixer who thrives in power circles, under pressure, and never backs down from a challenge. She always has a follow-up question and always demands a better answer. Raised to be ruthless by her powerful father, whose approval she craves, her strength and drive stemmed from her upbringing, even as she struggles with the personal life, she can never quite be just Olivia. She is always on and always has to be The Olivia Pope.

Frank Lucas of *'American Gangster'* is a tactful and disciplined leader who built a family enterprise that quietly outmaneuvered his competition. Known for his sharp strategy and relentless focus on working in his best interest, he rose to the top by being precise and calculated and learning from others.

Ray Donovan, in his own self-titled show, is a no-nonsense Hollywood fixer who always delivers. Despite a gritty past and a broken family, he protects his own at all costs, leads his siblings, and holds everything together, even as he wrestles with destructive habits behind the scenes.

What am I getting at here? These characters resonate deeply with me because I see parts of myself in each of them. Like Raymond Reddington I believe in strategy without explanation, influence, and using connections for a greater purpose. Like Olivia Pope, I carry a heavy load and move with confidence in powerful spaces and never back down from challenges, even if I have to end the night sipping wine and eating popcorn. Like Ray Donovan, I take on the role of protector and leader, constantly overwhelmed, making sure those I care about are safe while keeping things together under pressure. And like Frank Lucas, I move with precision, discipline, and a focus on building something that lasts and always want to make sure it's the purest version and I'm never too arrogant when I do it.

I keep them on my vision board, as odd as it may seem, because they remind me of the traits I already have and the ones I'm still reaching for and defining. More importantly, I want you to ask yourself: who are the characters that mirror your strengths? Who do you look at and say, "That's me, that's the energy I bring into the world"? Find them, study them, and let them remind you of what you're capable of.

I spent some time breaking down the board with you because I needed to bring you into my world so you could understand how deep my vision runs, how I see myself, and what I see for myself. Vision is what puts you on a Mission. I thumbtacked this vision board to my wall and went to work every single day. I clocked in every day, and when I looked to my right, it was looking at me. Every day I went to a job I didn't want to be at the vision was there. When I ate breakfast, it was looking at me. My mind subconsciously needed to make this my mission, and so I did.

I was consistent since August 2022, and at the publication of this book here are my results:

Hear me clearly, to this day:

- I am living the most authentic life and allowing my inner child uninhibited freedom.
- I have ended the toxic relationship with my father for my inner peace with no contact.
- I am debt free with an amazing credit score and pursuing financial freedom.
- I am a certified neuroscientist coach and an IKIGAI coach.
- I have contacts and wear them as I feel and with ease.
- I relocated to California as a permanent resident and live in a townhome.
- I was working from home at a job I enjoyed as a leader making the most money I ever have – until now, because I resigned upon releasing this project!

- I completed the single remaining class needed to get my Bachelor's degree, which I postponed for the last 15 years.
- I have set firm boundaries and ended relationships that don't serve me in life.
- I have new traditions with family, such as yearly cabin trips and overseas vacations.
- I finally have a growing stock portfolio, Roth IRA, and a Trust.
- I have a beautiful, thriving snake plant in my window, growing alongside others.
- I have an extensive wardrobe that I enjoy wearing, and my living environment evokes peace
- I have made new connections, new deals, and built my business empire.
- My consulting firm Inovision, operates across several states.
- I am looking at real estate to purchase my first multi-unit rental property.
- The book I've been thinking about since 2012 is in your hands right now!

I AM UNSTOPPABLE! There is nothing special about me except for the fact that I am the dream! Here's the funny thing about a dream, all it needs to do is step into the physical and just one step in this plane makes the dream reality. One step makes the vision a mission. I took one step, and then another, and then another. Now, I'm unstoppable.

I'm rooting for you! I'm yelling from the sideline like T'Challa's mother in Black Panther during his fight "Show them who you are!!!" When this happens for you my friend and you start to take up space in every room, people will respond accordingly. Your declaration followed up with delivery takes the air out of the lungs of naysayers. That's the space you take up in a room. Big space for your big ideas and your big plate! We hate small plates just like we hate small minds, don't we?

You know what the onlooking crowd says on all my social posts now when I share my living experiences? "You're living your best life!"

Damn right, and what's the response we give them? Same as before – I AM UNSTOPPABLE! We were consistent and we believed in the theory that we deserved it.

Always Moore, nothing less – and let the work do the rest. In the words of my late loved one...

"May my works speak for me."
– Uncle V.

CHAPTER 13

Serious or Delirious?

The journey you are embarking on requires you to graduate from trying to convince people that you are who you are. You are springing into the place of a producer and that is going to force others to second-guess you. It's not entirely their fault; they watched you second-guess yourself countless times, so they don't know whether to fully buy into this version of you yet. However, the way your confidence and consistency will flow it is going to draw a drastic contrast to that of the life you were experiencing under your limiting beliefs. Be fair warned that making that switch will have you prioritizing the things that mean most to you and pursuing them at any cost.

To a common-place person who allows any obstacle to stop them, your drive and tenacity, once you become unstoppable, will be shocking. Others will likely inquire about how serious and committed you are to the overall goal. If you choose to lay out your full vision, some may think you are delusional or just flat-out stupid. Prepare yourself to watch others try to derail you or jump ship once you take off. This next phase is not going to require only consistency from you, but commitment.

You will need to over-commit to everything you have planned. Commitment is tying yourself to the journey and owning all the steps and stops in between. If you have been brave enough to launch anything whatsoever, then see it through. All your plans and postponements deserve it. Make a lifelong commitment whenever you present your passion to the world, to give it everything that is within you.

If this is your first time starting a business, creating a unique good or service, packaging your creative talent, or adding value to the entrepreneurial marketplace, then welcome.

There is a part of the process where you have branded yourself as the person who delivers a certain caliber of content in a specific and unique way. Your entire audience is counting on you to do exactly what you said you would. The distinction between you and your brand should be seamless as it relates to its value, but both should appear flawless. After all, you have been working on this in your mind forever, and it has a foolproof plan. Commitment is crucial to sustaining what you have finally given yourself over to. When an idea is released from an individual and into the world, it takes on a life of its own. Although it still requires guidance, growth, and refinement, the owner and driver of that new idea must remain committed to its maturation. The beginning does not dictate the end, and so giving up too soon or moving too quickly will be a fatal mistake to the success of your endeavor.

Here's a tip: don't listen to everyone on the sideline, because **not all input is profitable or warranted for the final output.**

You have planned your work, now work your plan. No matter what you do, stay committed to building and improving your systems and processes, so that you have what it takes to go the distance. Read that sentence again – you are no longer perfecting; you are building, adapting, implementing, and improving. The goal is for your contribution to this world to have a lasting impact on anyone who encounters you. You can only do that if you have a vision to grow and scale whatever it is you are putting out. This is the last step of your process—growth. You quite literally are ready to grow up. You have already proven that you **know**; you took the steps to **show**, and now it's time to **grow** and never stop.

Focus In

Growth is uncomfortable, especially when you are doing something new that those around you may not fully understand. When you grow into one thing, you outgrow the other. You cannot take both.

What are you more committed to? Your past or your future? You have to ask yourself this. When your language and level of conversations begin to change, you will lose some people, but what are you gaining in return? See, I've been around a great deal of non-starters and do-it-laters for a long time, and that kept me feeling good. It poisoned me slowly because anything I did, even if it was just resting in my potential or sharing a plan, they were in awe and ready to celebrate. Get away from people who keep celebrating your small plate. I hate small plates. And you need to stop acting like you aren't hungry for everything you've cast on your vision board. You deserve all that, but only if you're committed. Will you do what it takes when it comes time to cut the leisure time and kill the time wasters?

Your main goal is to develop a killer focus that can't be stopped by anything happening around you. **Your focus should be on your business, not your busyness**. Just because you are moving doesn't mean you are being productive – so be intentional. Allow me to reiterate that no one can effectively focus on more than one thing at a time. So, if that means devoting certain days for your marketing vs structural changes, then so be it. The focus on the details of whatever you put into the world to ensure it accurately represents who you are and what you envisioned is supreme. No one will know the intricacies of your business like you and if you aren't patching the holes then who will? The quickest way to get distracted from your goal is to start hyper-focusing on the responses of other people who haven't contributed or built anything lasting themselves. There comes a time to take their feedback into consideration but don't commit to trying to please everyone when you are just starting. Stay focused on your overall mission.

Marathon Mindset

That radical decision to get out of your head and serious about your mission, brings more with it than just launching and introducing yourself to the world. You must commit to the long game. This is a mindset shift, and we will call it the *Marathon Mindset*. (Shout out to the late Nipsey Hussle.)

It is said that 90% of new businesses fail in their first year because people often want quick success, when in fact, it's a marathon. I blame the glamorization of achievements without recognizing the struggles faced in the mud. I've seen entrepreneurs who leave their jobs abruptly, without a commitment to the marathon or a solid strategy, only to end up selling their business for a paycheck. Taking on any customer who offers a few dollars is never a wise decision, as it may help keep things afloat temporarily. Since they may need money, they abandon their plan and vision, chasing after short-term gains, and eventually face burnout along with the normal business challenges. It's never wise to be hasty in quitting your day job, as it serves as your main investor in your new venture. If your primary cash flow comes from your 9-5, what sense does it make to abandon that unless you can match or exceed that income through your business or other means? Don't let short-term excitement cause you to forfeit the long-term benefits of trusting the process.

I recall speaking to one of my friends, a well-known graphic artist Nick Rich, who would share with me the horror stories of certain clients he had worked with. They often had these outlandish requests that, for the scope of work and their de-

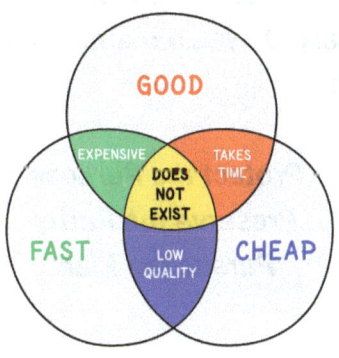

mands, simply didn't fit. I remember him breaking it down to me the best way he could, which was using a graphic that I later learned was well-known when it comes to the service industry and consumers.

As the line goes: "You can choose between cheap, fast, and good but you can only choose two."

The principle I want you to apply is to always keep the good supreme. Keep it at the top because you have a good idea, a solid business model, and a commitment to delivering good results. Don't go get desperate now when executing and sacrifice good for anything less than, because then greatness will forever evade you. I'm warning you of the game now. If you see your peers pumping out content, they may be consistent but ask if it's good. It doesn't have to be perfect, but is it intentional and on purpose? If you allow your audience or arenas to push you into only delivering fast and cheap to prove you belong, then you have abandoned what made you good and entered the valley of low-quality production. That is not where you deserve to live, because your competition is not others, but rather yourself. On the other hand, if you let them demand all three simultaneously, you must draw the boundary to keep the good pure. Here is a grounding technique to help you revisit setting that boundary. Do you remember that PTP mantra from earlier? Say it with me.

Protect the Purpose
Preserve the Purity
Pursue the Plan

This is how you maintain the good in all that you do in order to ascend to the great. Remind yourself that in all that you put your hand to in this marathon the end goal is bigger than the small prize. I must continue to protect, preserve and pursue to map out my legacy with the imprint I hope to leave on the world. Always ensure that your account for your actions and only put out what you would be proud to claim ownership of in the world.

How about another "P" word? **Patience.** The road you are now walking on requires you to have developed a high tolerance level for organizational challenges and be patient with a host of things outside of your control. This is the last part of what makes you unstoppable. You are sturdy and solid, no matter what the outside conditions. If, for example, you have a five-year plan, you are not concerned about some hiccups after one and a half years. Being committed to the long-term plan will allow you to have a big plate with each piece receiving its proper focus at the necessary time, so that it can be devoured and digested well, as you adjust accordingly along the way.

What changed my mentality was to think about how to execute as if I had already completed my race. Sitting in my room, I was banging my head against the desk, thinking about how to make all of what I wanted to do make sense, and it struck me. Marvel Cinematic Universe (MCU). The MCU has produced amazing films and media using phases that span years. The beauty is that the move prior is lining up the move after all within its respective phase. I have never been overwhelmed by all that Marvel has set out to accomplish, because each movie or show they release always ties into their overall vision for the phase they are in.

They are not hurried, panicking, or bothered if fans react and request one character or installment over another. The executives at Marvel have a Marathon Mindset. Each film and show will come out in its expected time and it will build all into the entire cinematic universe to show great purpose and symmetry in each installment. I adopted that when I thought about a marathon mindset. I said to myself I don't have to do all this right away and no one needs to know it's all coming or when it's coming. As long as I know how everything will play out and give appropriate time for growth, testing, and improvements along the way I can follow a clear plan and reach an expected end. By the time I'm finished running a five-year plan the audience will grow to expect nothing but excellence from me. It won't be because I'm the best in one specific field, but I am consistent with staying on brand, and I am committed to the long-term vision and success.

Do not fall into the temptation of getting lost in immediate results, be it successes of failures. Just because your friends and family know that you've got motion, and perhaps you gained a few followers, it doesn't mean it's time to kick back. Ask any business owner you know, it's usually our friends and family who don't support us past the initial hype of us stepping off the porch and launching. They are not your customers, so please think bigger than your circle. A marathon mindset knows that even with 3,000 outside followers, we can't expect all of them or even 20% of them to translate their following to active engagement or support that can be quantified. The marathon mindset doesn't support you stumbling over short-term results and floundering over small failures. When you are serious about what it is you do, your commitment will be evident, and you will think with the end in mind. Stay the course.

I want to challenge you to think with the end in mind, with a long-term plan, even with your shorter interim steps. It's completely fine to tell yourself you will take two years to grow one arm of your business while building another funnel to flow into something else on the back end. The goal is that whatever you unleash in this world can grow to be sustainable and function without you dedicating all your time to it.

Finally, you must prioritize investing in and connecting with like-minded communities above all else. This is not something to overlook, as you will need those encouragement and support systems as you fail forward. Your growth depends not only on what you know but also on who you know. We all remember how the job market has been in recent years, right? Qualified job seekers from different fields applied to hundreds of jobs and remained unemployed because we are now in an age where community and connections can be the key to getting your foot in the door. Relationships are valuable currency, as we discussed earlier, but now that you are a producer, it's about community and becoming part of one.

Start Something New

It's invaluable to think about what tips, tricks, strategies, and hacks you learn from having like-minded mission-forward people surrounding you. It can and will drastically reduce the hard work and headaches you face when going at it alone. Learning from other people's experiences before repeating their mistakes or navigating nuances in your industry and with certain players. Whatever you must do to find and continue in a community that is all headed the same way, factor that into your execution. If it looks like joining active clubs/groups, attending networking events, being part of a mastermind, or just building with those in your industry, then do it.

The language and long game of true winners is about growing, protecting, and sustaining. That's the true GPS you want to follow. We are all learning together, and if you can establish a community that will help you refine your process to **KNOW-SHOW-GROW** repeatedly, then latch onto them and don't let go!

My heart's desire for decades has been to have something like this. I've never had a business mentor, and I don't come from an entrepreneurial family. When I share this with you, I'm saying that for some of us, we are used to going it alone and figuring things out as we go. We are pioneers and first-timers, so the pressure and inexperience are all present. There are valuable lessons to be learned from this; however, time would be better spent elsewhere if we could avoid all the trial and error. Many times, I wanted to be guided, mentored, or part of a group of go-getters who were just as creative, ambitious, and excited as I was—to celebrate success and share strategies. I've come close at times, but those spaces often disappeared or turned into strange marketing funnels for new sales channels. As I mentioned, I value au-

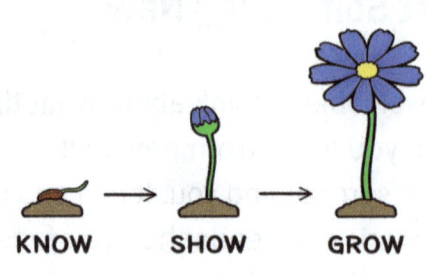

thenticity because I believe it's the highest form of truth, and I wasn't finding it outside a Business Chamber of Commerce or half-dead Facebook group.

They say if you don't see what you desire in the world, perhaps it is because you are supposed to create it. As fearful as I was for a long time about being perceived in certain ways, it has kept me from both giving to others and receiving. As part of my contribution, along with this book and all my life's work and guidance, I want to make sure we go from being total strangers to friends, ultimately to family. Community builds family, and that is why I have created the **KNOW-SHOW-GROW Lifestyle Community,** also known as the KSG Lifestyle Community. This is a member-only, hand selected, premium group of individuals who are highly motivated and committed to success, striving for daily exponential growth together.

The group will meet regularly and engage in ongoing discussion while sharing lessons, receiving coaching and trainings, exchanging tips, access to free resources, and much more. We don't hoard or gatekeep, we build each other. We are marathon runners and we run together. What we know, we show, and what we show we use to grow – one to another. That's the KSG Lifestyle. To learn more and be invited in where you belong, visit me at iamdantemoore.com to get plugged in.

Family, I can start with me and provide to you all that you need here to be successful, but at the end of it all, this is about you. Who and what I am is just one person, but together we are a force, and we can change the world if we pool our resources and talent and create an ecosystem that fosters and forces us to grow what we know and already show. Join us as you have joined me on this amazing journey because when it's all done and the curtain closes for you, what more is there left? You must start with yourself in order to end with them.

That is legacy.

CHAPTER 14

End With Them

Relationships are the fabric of everything we do. When I really grasped this, I put everything into being successful with people and relationships. It's why I became an Insight Extraction Coach as it helped me understand myself and others better for growth. I wanted to start with myself and improving from the inside out. My reality was that if I can be built up and execute, the overflow of everything I'm doing in my life will act as an overflow to directly impact and benefit those connected to me. Success for you should not just be about you launching an idea you had and making it happen. That is a goal to chart success, however ultimately it should speak to the good you have put into the world by your contribution.

Executing eliminates excuses. Instead of thinking about every scenario that could go wrong and overanalyzing pathways to failure – just start. When you do so be committed to bringing your full effort and attention to all your unique insights to apply them.

We are coming to the end of our time together, and yet it feels like we are just getting started. All we've been doing this whole time is perspective shifting, cold plunging, and mind hacking your psyche to get you back in control of your life. When you are purposed to do a great work, it doesn't feel like an arduous task; it is a dutiful delight. What else would I be doing with my time? Exchanging it for money and living someone else's dream at the expense of my own time and heart's desires? We know now that we have opted out of that American Nightmare. We operate now on the Theory of Moore.

Much of what you've read here might need revisiting, and that's okay as long as you apply it. Don't let this be just another good book you put on the shelf and recommend to a friend. This is a rebrand guide and blueprint for rebirth, as well as a tool to help you get out of your own way. I hope you see that whether we use history, movie scenes, science, psychology, economics, comedy, anecdotes, study of human behavior, anthropology, metaphors, hip-hop lyrics, real-life scenarios, etymology, or just straightforward talk, we can get the same point across. I will use the most effective media and methods to share this information, making sure you can receive and keep it. All of this only matters if you take it and use it; that's when this becomes a win for me.

Creating this book was looked at more as a labor of love and a necessary requirement than it was considered as work. I was speaking from my heart, drawing on my experience, using my intellect, and addressing a very particular audience who knows me, and I know them. We see each other because we are one another, just at different points. In this way, everything you read and experience here with me through our time together is only an overflow of what happens when I am in alignment. The same is true for you. When you operate according to what you are called to do and be, the things you produce and create are going to be an offspring of who you are and what you possess. This is how you start with you to end with them. I modeled that for you by taking you on the journey and showing you what it takes.

There are those who will try to shortcut this process and skip the hard work. They don't have the authenticity that you do or life experiences, but they have money and can just copy what others are doing. They won't see the same results, nor will they have the same lasting success. Remember, nothing worth keeping comes quickly. You know what it's like to toil. I know what it is like. When we leave our end audience, we leave them with the best of what we have because we've put our entire soul into it. So, when you create, if you've done this right you can rest in knowing that because you got yourself in order first, that the end user is getting the best representation of what you have to offer. Whether that is your service, your advice, your product, your time, or whatever you give to the world. There is a method to the madness, and we don't build fast to crash quickly. We remain intentional, graceful, and thankful as we pursue our wildest imaginations.

You may have started off like me as a Planning Procrastinating Perfectionist, but from this day forward, you are no more. I would like to submit to you that the only thing I want to see next is Passion Projects Prevailing & Profiting. Oh, and did I mention that's on *Period*!

In all seriousness though, I have modeled everything I am telling you in this book throughout this book. We are at the end, and the book ends where I started when I first thought to write it, which was hoping I could move out to California, and here I am. I told you to start with you, and I have done that hard work, which is the heart work, and created ways for others to discover themselves as well. We have walked through how you deserve more than a small plate, and you have to say to yourself, "I AM THE ASSET" and begin to invest in yourself accordingly. I have partnered with you for your growth in helping to assist you through all this because this is not the end of you and I, this is the beginning.

I see you as family, and I enjoy eating with my family and building with them as they succeed, and I succeed! I'm not just leaving you with nice inspirational words, but practical tools and resources to get jump-started today! What you do from here is up to you, but you can never say I didn't give you my all so that we could continue to labor to change the world together. Some of you don't need anything else – you are ready to activate, and that brings me so much joy, and I can't wait to hear your story. Share it with us as I've already introduced you to the KSG Lifestyle Community to continue in unison with you as we champion our growth together. However, if you need it, here are a few more ways you can benefit from the material and how I can partner with you beyond this book to help you make it all make sense and come to life.

The Hard Work is the Heart Work Method

If you are interested in understanding more about yourself, starting with you, and who exactly you are and how you operate, this is for you. I had the amazing privilege as an Insight Extraction Coach to work directly with The HWork2 Method Inc. as they developed a concise and tailored roadmap based on my personal feedback. It's easy to read about others and look at charts, but you need something interactive and distinct to assists you to identify your unique person. However, if you're unsure what that looks like, let's get more specific!

The Hard Work is the Heart Work Method is an intentional series of assessments, cognitive tests, critical questions, and thought-provoking tools designed to unearth who you are and what you possess, providing you with tailored results. Apart from your standard work personality profile, this dossier, when completed, will leave you feeling confident in finding your inner person and extracting their full purpose, enabling you to embark on future pursuits. This is by far the simplest and most life-changing, insightful work I've completed in getting to where I am today. The assessments aren't long and drawn out, the results are clear and applicable, and each feels different. This is where clarity emerges. **Visit hwork2.com to unpack yourself today.**

I Am The A$$ET – Online course

For those of you who understand what you are and what you possess, and you want to take it to the next level of how to apply it fully for yourself or how to start and launch a business from A-Z, make your brand stand out, or create content that sticks -this is designed for you.

I AM THE ASSET is more than an affirmation but a self-paced course designed to give you step-by-step processes to translate the core of who you are into the creation that can produce currency. Keeping YOU central, these guided modules with application steps help you eliminate the guesswork and get the momentum to move towards actualizing the framework to monetize myself. You are the most significant asset; you just have to know how to position yourself to win. We help teach that in this course through two different tracks and at two separate paces, so no one is left behind. **Meet us over at theassetcourse.com**

INOVISION – Where innovation meets vision

Perhaps you read this book, and you already know who you are and have things running, but you were at a dry spell for a moment; it happens to all of us. Now that you are back, if you need assistance via consulting or help with any specialized projects or creative campaigns, we've got your back!

INOVISION is a consulting firm I founded several years ago where innovation meets vision. We consult, we coach, we create—helping people like you turn bold ideas into strategies and real results. If you've ever felt stuck between what you see for yourself and how to make it happen, that is enough to add to the delay. That's where INOVISION comes in—bridging the gap between vision and execution, giving you the clarity, structure, and creative support to finally move forward. Our team provides hands-on guidance, tailored to your level, for a step-by-step approach to execution.

If this feels aligned with what you need and you are ready to move vision into action, **let's connect at *inovisionconsulting.com***

Those are my shameless plugs—and when I say shameless, there is nothing, I'm telling you to do that I don't do myself. I exist to do exactly what this book has done and reveal to you all that lies within its pages. For the last 16+ years, I've been speaking in this same exact way to anyone who will listen, so why would I stop now? I can only be me, and that's what I've given you: all of me.

However, there is no shame because this is all my passion, and remember, **passion projects often prevail and yield profit**. That's what they deserve to do because the secret sauce, a passion project, is often very closely aligned, if not directly in stride, with your purpose. You've done it for free, on a small scale, and with the wrong crowd for too long. There is no shame in placing it right where it needs to be –in the hands of the doers!

> ***More needs to be done than said.***

When you deliver to your core audience, consumer, or end user, have you thought about what you are leaving them with? That's what this chapter is here to show you.

> ***I was told a long time ago, "Dante, whenever you leave a room, leave it with the residue of value dripped all over your shoes as you walk out."***

I want to leave value everywhere I go so that someone can look down at my footprints and see that those marks are worth studying and examining. This is the legacy-building work right here and how you begin it. People often think it primarily happens with having children, but it can also be everyday social interactions that give birth to new life and hope in ordinary people. I want you to think bigger than what you once considered big. Once you start executing and reaching your desired targets, think about what you can leave behind after your initial introduction to showcase your value to them. You want others to continue benefiting from all that you have to offer. Some of that can be free content and updates; others could be exclusive members-only deals, or maybe it's building a new client relationship. I've gone on to hire people I've met through companies I've started to continue adding value to their lives. How that looks for you could differ from others, but make sure that once you've done your work, you leave a legacy and are never forgotten. Don't be forgettable. Leave so much value that people call you the plug and know where to come back for a re-up. That's how you end with them—and end well.

I am proud that you have reached this place and this moment! Let's make magic and continue to set milestones as we build a lasting legacy that blazes trails for future generations.

I am Dante Moore, your coach, peer, mentor, and friend, and I'm grateful to be in the same space as you on this earth. Let's win and win big because we are no longer stuck in our own heads with all that could be; we are truly at rest, knowing that we are **finally stepping into our lives!**

About the Author

Dante Moore knows what it feels like to be stuck. Hailing from the city of Philadelphia a place riddled with hustlers and talent for years he was the planning, procrastinating perfectionist who slept on his own potential. Always playing the background, while propelling others forward, and overcomplicating his own initiatives. Through much experience, missteps, and self-discovery, he learned how to fully embrace who he is authentically to pull clarity from chaos and move into action — and now, as an Insight Extraction Coach he helps others do the same.

He is more than just an entrepreneur, strategist, author and speaker. When he isn't coaching or consulting, Dante is an avid foodie who loves exploring new eateries with vibrant dishes matching a visually aesthetic ambiance. He enjoys diving into big ideas and deep conversations, while finding alignment with those in his circle. He is a die-hard Philadelphia Eagles fan who loves to rep his city! Outside of that, he finds joy at an occasional live concert or comedy show, spending time with his family, and connecting with those who are chasing purpose and impact. His passion is simple: helping other human beings break free from the constraints of their own mind with a pattern of new thinking and habits, in order to help them finally start living the life they've been dreaming about.